Folens
History in Action 5

Author:
Karen Cooksey

Acknowledgements

The author and publishers would like to thank Valerie Price for help with research and the following for permission to reproduce the following copyright material:

p.6 Hulton-Deutsch Collection/CORBIS
p.10 from http://learningcurve.pro.gov.uk, National Archives
p.11 adapted from 'A well conducted factory' *The Penny Magazine*, 16 November 1833, no. 104
p.23 *Life as We Have Known It* (1931), Margaret Llewelyn Davies (ed.), London: Hogarth Press
p.29 Ordnance Survey 1:500 1888 map of Castleford from www.arch.wyjs.org.uk/AdvSrv/RomanWeb/images/rw36.jpg, with permission of the West Yorkshire Archaeology Service
p.34 adapted from *Intelligencer*, 13 January 1831, quoted on www.mtholyoke.edu
p.45 graphs adapted from House of Commons Library. Research paper 99/111, 21 December 1999, 'A Century of Change: trends in UK statistics since 1900'
p.46 CORBIS
p.47 miners' strike, Betmann/CORBIS
p.47 text adapted from BBCNewsatbbcnews.co.uk
p.47 graph adapted from House of Commons Library. Research paper 99/111, 21 December 1999, 'A Century of Change: trends in UK statistics since 1900'
p.50 Lajpat Rai Vij adapted from biography, Liverpool Museum
p.50 Leroy Logan adapted from Jamaica Information Service
p.55 Roger Bannister, Betmann/CORBIS
p.55 central Manchester, Reuters/CORBIS
p.55 1966 World Cup, Hulton-Deutsch Collection/CORBIS
p.55 Prince Charles and Lady Dianna, Quadrillion/CORBIS
p.55 men on the moon, Ressmeyer/CORBIS
p.55 test-tube baby, Bettmann/CORBIS
p.55 Greenham Common, Bettmann/CORBIS
p.55 decimal day, Hulton-Deutsch Collection/CORBIS
p.55 funeral of Diana, Princess of Wales, Julian Calder/CORBIS
p.55 Queen Elizabeth II's coronation, Bettmann/CORBIS
p.57 1950s shop, Bettmann/CORBIS.
p.57 2000 shopping centre, Laurie Shaw
p.59 Frigidaire
p.59 Dunlop Vynolay
p.59 adapted from MT
p.61 adapted from Cambridge Introduction to the History of Mankind 'Europe Finds the World' by Trevor Cairns, Cambridge: Cambridge University Press
p.65 illustration adapted from *Age of Exploration*, New York: Time Life Books
p.75 adapted from Barlowe's letter to Walter Raleigh, cited in *The Principall Voyages, Traffiques, and Discourses of the English Nations (1599–1600)*, reprinted in Albert Bushnell Hart (ed.), *American History Told by Contemporaries* (New York, 1898), Volume 1
p.79 redrawn from John White's paintings; (top) *The protected village life* (middle) *The Manner of Their Fishing*; (bottom) The Crops and Fruit of a Fertile Continent

Contents

Introduction

Folens History in Action meets the requirements for the National Curriculum in England and Wales, and is compatible with the schemes of work published in England by the Qualifications and Curriculum Authority (QCA). It will work best when combined with a range of history resources such as books, photos, videos, artefacts and, for some topics, interviews with visitors.

Aims of Folens History in Action

The overall aim of the book is that children should: develop knowledge and understanding of significant periods, people and events in history; learn to interpret historical evidence and understand that knowledge about history is subject to interpretation.

The aim of individual activities is to provide opportunities for children to engage with the subject matter and process it in some way, such as matching, sequencing, using information to draw, write a specific form of text, or label a diagram. Children's thinking skills will develop better if they are allowed to verbalise their thought processes in pairs or small groups; most of the activities are designed to be used in this way.

The Structure of Folens History in Action

The book is divided into four units, each covering a history topic suitable for Year 5 and Year 6, as defined by the schemes of work. Each unit contains a term's work; it is expected that teachers will choose three of the topics for the year.

The first unit will help children to appreciate the attitudes as well as the circumstances governing young lives in the Victorian period, understand that they changed over time and compare them to their own lives today. In the second unit on Victorian times, background information is provided on those aspects of development likely to have affected local communities, but children are presented with an opportunity to develop knowledge and skills for carrying out their own research. In the third unit children learn to use a variety of sources to describe changes in Britain since 1948 and to identify and sequence the most significant events and developments. The section 'Comparing the Decades' provides a starting point for children's own investigation of either one aspect of life since 1948, or one decade. 'Tudor Exploration' is a more knowledge-based unit and provides activities that will enable children to understand, and enjoy learning about, significant features of Tudor navigation and exploration.

The units are further divided into sub-topics, each starting with a teachers' page. The teachers' page contains notes to explain and provide background for the activities which follow.

gives the objectives covered in the activity sheets

gives a brief introduction to the topic and information relevant to the activities

suggests a useful way in which teachers can prepare the class for each activity

brief notes on how to deliver the activity which forms the main part of the lesson, and which the majority of children will complete

a suggestion as to how to make the activity suitable for children at a lower level of achievement

an idea for a more challenging activity which can be given to higher achieving or enthusiastic children after they have completed the main activity

an idea for rounding up and consolidating the learning after all the activities referred to on the teachers' page have been completed

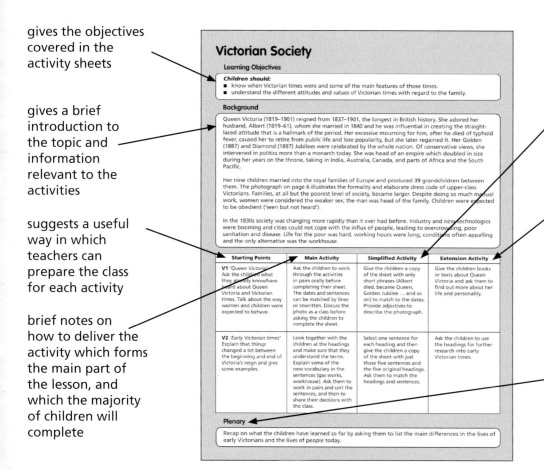

Victorian Society

Learning Objectives

Children should:
- know when Victorian times were and some of the main features of those times.
- understand the different attitudes and values of Victorian times with regard to the family.

Background

Queen Victoria (1819–1901) reigned from 1837–1901, the longest in British history. She adored her husband, Albert (1819–61), whom she married in 1840 and he was influential in creating the straight-laced attitude that is a hallmark of the period. Her excessive mourning for him, after he died of typhoid fever, caused her to retire from public life and lose popularity, but she later regained it. Her Golden (1887) and Diamond (1897) Jubilees were celebrated by the whole nation. Of conservative views, she intervened in politics more than a monarch today. She was head of an empire which doubled in size during her years on the throne, taking in India, Australia, Canada, and parts of Africa and the South Pacific.

Her nine children married into the royal families of Europe and produced 39 grandchildren between them. The photograph on page 6 illustrates the formality and elaborate dress code of upper-class Victorians. Families, at all but the poorest level of society, became larger. Despite doing so much menial work, women were considered the weaker sex; the man was head of the family. Children were expected to be obedient ('seen but not heard').

In the 1830s society was changing more rapidly than it ever had before. Industry and new technologies were booming and cities could not cope with the influx of people, leading to overcrowding, poor sanitation and disease. Life for the poor was hard, working hours were long, conditions often appalling and the only alternative was the workhouse.

Starting Points	Main Activity	Simplified Activity	Extension Activity
V1 *'Queen Victoria'* Ask the children what they already know/have heard about Queen Victoria and Victorian times. Talk about the way women and children were expected to behave.	Ask the children to work through the activities in pairs orally before completing their sheet. The dates and sentences can be matched by lines or rewritten. Discuss the photo as a class before asking the children to complete the sheet.	Give the children a copy of the sheet with only short phrases (Albert died, became Queen, Golden Jubilee … and so on) to match to the dates. Provide adjectives to describe the photograph.	Give the children books or texts about Queen Victoria and ask them to find out more about her life and personality.
V2 *'Early Victorian times'* Explain that things changed a lot between the beginning and end of Victoria's reign and give some examples.	Look together with the children at the headings and make sure that they understand the terms. Explain some of the new vocabulary in the sentences (gas works, workhouse). Ask them to work in pairs and sort the sentences, and then to share their decisions with the class.	Select one sentence for each heading and then give the children a copy of the sheet with just those five sentences and the five original headings. Ask them to match the headings and sentences.	Ask the children to use the headings for further research into early Victorian times.

Plenary

Recap on what the children have learned so far by asking them to list the main differences in the lives of early Victorians and the lives of people today.

Victorian Society

Learning Objectives

Children should:
- know when Victorian times were and some of the main features of those times.
- understand the different attitudes and values of Victorian times with regard to the family.

Background

Queen Victoria (1819–1901) reigned from 1837–1901, the longest in British history. She adored her husband, Albert (1819–61), whom she married in 1840 and he was influential in creating the straight-laced attitude that is a hallmark of the period. Her excessive mourning for him, after he died of typhoid fever, caused her to retire from public life and lose popularity, but she later regained it. Her Golden (1887) and Diamond (1897) Jubilees were celebrated by the whole nation. Of conservative views, she intervened in politics more than a monarch today. She was head of an empire which doubled in size during her years on the throne, taking in India, Australia, Canada, and parts of Africa and the South Pacific.

Her nine children married into the royal families of Europe and produced 39 grandchildren between them. The photograph on page 6 illustrates the formality and elaborate dress code of upper-class Victorians. Families, at all but the poorest level of society, became larger. Despite doing so much manual work, women were considered the weaker sex; the man was head of the family. Children were expected to be obedient ('seen but not heard').

In the 1830s society was changing more rapidly than it ever had before. Industry and new technologies were booming and cities could not cope with the influx of people, leading to overcrowding, poor sanitation and disease. Life for the poor was hard, working hours were long, conditions often appalling and the only alternative was the workhouse.

Starting Points	Main Activity	Simplified Activity	Extension Activity
V1 *'Queen Victoria'* Ask the children what they already know/have heard about Queen Victoria and Victorian times. Talk about the way women and children were expected to behave.	Ask the children to work through the activities in pairs orally before completing their sheet. The dates and sentences can be matched by lines or rewritten. Discuss the photo as a class before asking the children to complete the sheet.	Give the children a copy of the sheet with only short phrases (Albert died, became Queen, Golden Jubilee … and so on) to match to the dates. Provide adjectives to describe the photograph.	Give the children books or texts about Queen Victoria and ask them to find out more about her life and personality.
V2 *'Early Victorian times'* Explain that things changed a lot between the beginning and end of Victoria's reign and give some examples.	Look together with the children at the headings and make sure that they understand the terms. Explain some of the new vocabulary in the sentences (gas works, workhouse). Ask them to work in pairs and sort the sentences, and then to share their decisions with the class.	Select one sentence for each heading and then give the children a copy of the sheet with just those five sentences and the five original headings. Ask them to match the headings and sentences.	Ask the children to use the headings for further research into early Victorian times.

Plenary

Recap on what the children have learned so far by asking them to list the main differences in the lives of early Victorians and the lives of people today.

Queen Victoria

- Match the dates to the events in Queen Victoria's life.

<table>
<tr><td>1819</td><td>Albert died from typhoid fever; Victoria grieved for ten years</td></tr>
<tr><td>1837</td><td>a national celebration for her Golden Jubilee</td></tr>
<tr><td>1840</td><td>died</td></tr>
<tr><td>1861</td><td>married her cousin, Prince Albert of Saxe-Coburg-Gotha; they had nine children</td></tr>
<tr><td>1887</td><td>born at Kensington Palace in London</td></tr>
<tr><td>1901</td><td>took the throne after the death of her uncle, William IV</td></tr>
</table>

- What do you notice about:

The size of the family? _____

The children's clothes? _____

_____

The adult's clothes? _____

_____

- Why do you think Queen Victoria is wearing black?

_____

- How would you describe the posture and expressions of the Royal Family?

_____

_____

FOLENS HISTORY IN ACTION 5 © Folens (copiable page)

Early Victorian times

● Cut out and match the sentences under the correct heading.

Work	Health and housing	The law	Transport	Empire

Many children died before the age of five.

Many adults died by the age of 40.

If there were no railway poor people walked; rich people used horses and a carriage.

Many textile factories were built.

Many mines for extracting coal and iron were opened.

There were new gas works, shipyards, and factories.

Britain ruled over other people in India and Africa.

Lots of new railway lines were being built.

People could be put to death for many crimes, including stealing something worth more than £2.

Thousands of people were leaving the countryside to work in the new factories.

There were not enough houses in the cities.

Poor people with no money had to go to the workhouse.

Child Labour

Learning Objectives

Children should:
- learn about the lives of working children in Victorian times.
- understand how ideas about childhood have changed.

Background

Before the industrial revolution, most children were expected to work on the land with their parents. Money that children earned was vital to the family budget and this continued to be the case as people moved to cities and factory jobs, but the long hours and poor conditions put them at a greater risk. Children were often 'apprenticed' to an employer, effectively signed over by their parents for a period of years. Other children had no parents and were taken from the workhouses. As children were paid less to work, there was an incentive for employers to use as many of them as possible.

State provision for education and welfare were very new ideas in the early Victorian period. 'The rich man in his castle, the poor man at his gate' described what many Victorians would accept as a God-given order. Even the more enlightened employers, like the one described on page 11, were not challenging this social order just making it more palatable. Children today need help to understand the change from these attitudes to modern ideas of equal opportunity and human rights.

Starting Points	Main Activity	Simplified Activity	Extension Activity
V3 *'Children at work'* Explain why children went to work (and had always worked) in Victorian times.	Discuss the pictures of the mines and the answers to the questions as a class, before asking the children to write. Ask them to discuss the other jobs in pairs and write answers on a separate sheet and then report back to the class.	Give the children a list of dangers or difficulties (your clothes could get caught in a machine, your back would ache, you might fall … and so on) and ask them to match the phrases to each of the five jobs pictured.	Ask the children to write, from the point of view of a Victorian, a 'handbill' (a popular way of expressing personal views in Victorian times) to give their opinion about child labour.
V4 *'Reports from the mines'* Remind the class about the type of work done by children in mines; recall the dangers and difficulties discussed in the previous lesson. Explain 'hurrier' as a job in the mines and 'stays' as a corset/bodice.	Make sure that the children know what information to look for and ask them to read the texts and complete as much of the table as they can. Allow time for them to compare answers, and then discuss these and other points of interest in the reports.	Give the children a copy of one of the texts with the information needed for the table already underlined. Ask them to fill in one row of the table.	Ask the children to write part of the report of the inspectors after interviewing these and other similar children. Give suggestions for paragraph headings (hours, conditions, clothes …).
V5 *'A good employer'* Explain that some employers looked after their workers, and that this was out of choice/ conscience, not because the law obliged them to.	Explain that the language of the report has been amended. Ask the children to read and underline key phrases that show how mill workers' lives are better than mineworkers'. Discuss this, and what the report does not say, before asking them to write.	Read the report with the children, and then give them a list of questions to answer. (Did the girls go to school? Was there a doctor? Did they have time to play? Could they go home? and so on)	Ask the children to list reasons why some Victorians, like this writer, were in favour of child workers. Give prompts: cost, type of work, beliefs about children, and beliefs about poor people.

Plenary

Hold a Victorian debate: ask the children who have prepared arguments in favour of child labour (extension activity for page 11) to represent one side and choose others to argue against. If possible, give the children Victorian dress to wear and make it clear that they are playing a role.

Children at work

- Look at these pictures of children working in coal mines.

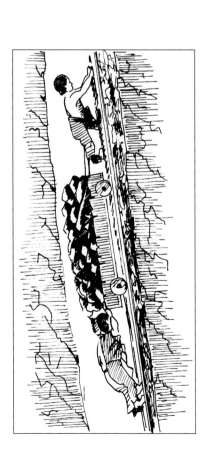

What made the work unpleasant and difficult?

_____

_____

Why was this work dangerous?

_____

_____

Here are some other jobs that children might have done. Write down some dangers or difficulties for each of these jobs:

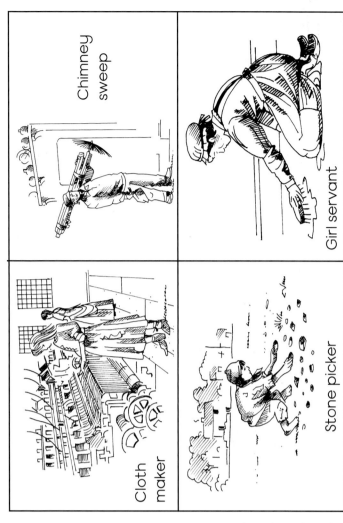

Chimney sweep

Cloth maker

Girl servant

Stone picker

- Describe the job the children are doing.

_____

_____

_____

_____

V3

Reports from the mines

These reports are from children who were interviewed by inspectors.

Esther Craven, aged 14

'… mother has been dead two years; I have one brother a hurrier, and a sister a hurrier, and a little one at home; father is a weaver … come here to work at seven, sometimes afore, never much after; I get my breakfast before I come, and bring my dinner with me, a piece of cake; when I go home I get milk and meal, sometimes potatoes; I do not know what time I go home, sometimes at three, four, five and six; I hurry in trousers bare-legged, and a pair of old stays … Joseph Ibbotson often beats us … I get many a time hurt my feet by hurrying; I get all the skin off my leg sometimes by the stones in the gate, and with the rail ends when they are loose; a pick struck me once and broke my finger; I cannot read or write; I never go much to Sunday-school, because I have no clothes fit to go in …'

George Bentley, aged 8

Has worked a year; … has 1s per day. He lives at South Normanton and has a mile and a half to walk to the pit. He breakfasts before he leaves home. Goes down half past six [a.m.] to eight [p.m.], one hour dinner … half days half past six to half past three or four, no dinner-hour allowed. He never works by night or Sunday. Has bread and fat for breakfast, bread, potatoes, and sometimes bacon for dinner, and bread and milk at night. He goes to the Ranter's Sunday School at Normanton, learns a b c.

● Fill in the table below.

	Hours of work per day	Food for: breakfast	dinner (midday)	supper (evening)	Education
Esther					
George					

FOLENS HISTORY IN ACTION 5 © Folens (copiable page)

A good employer

A few employers were concerned about their workers and provided better working conditions. These children were still working between eight and 12 hours a day.

In the factory of Mr. Wood about six hundred people, mainly girls, are employed. When we arrived it was the dinner-hour and the young people were playing in the open yard of the factory, like children out of school. The mill was as clean, as light, and as comfortable as a living-room, or rather as a series of living-rooms, for there are several floors filled with machinery. The children, in going back to their work, had not lost their cheerful look, but set about their tasks happily. Seats are provided for children who are not working. The little work-people seemed quite delighted to see their employer; their faces brightened up, and their eyes sparkled as he came near and spoke to them; indeed he appeared to be more like a father among them.

There is always a surplus number of children in the mill, so that they may be sent by turns to a school-room, where they learn to knit and to sew, as well as to read and to write. The reason given by their employer for teaching them knitting and needlework is because he had found that when girls, employed from an early age in a mill, were married, they did not know how to perform a wife's and a mother's duties and became idle gossips. A schoolmaster lives in, and Mr. Wood allows other poor children, besides those employed in his own mill, to attend the school. A doctor visits the factory weekly to examine the general health of the children, and attend to those who may be ill.

- List the things that these girls had to make their lives better than the children in the mines.

_____

_____

_____

The author of this report seems to be in favour of girls working in factories. Can you think of some things the report does not tell us. Write some questions you would like to ask.

Can the girls visit their families? _____

_____

_____

_____

Social Reform

Learning Objectives

Children should:
- learn about the work of Thomas Bernardo and Lord Shaftesbury.
- learn about some of the ways conditions improved for children in Victorian times.

Background

Thomas Bernardo and Lord Shaftesbury (born Anthony Ashley Cooper) were two of the most prominent of a number of earnest social reformers in Victorian times. They were both evangelical Christians, believing that it was not enough to preach, people's physical needs had also to be attended to. Bernardo worked exclusively for homeless and uneducated children. He was forward thinking for his time; his homes included children from ethnic minorities and those with disabilities. He was a pioneer of the fund raising methods used by charities today.

Shaftesbury campaigned in Parliament for a range of social causes, including treatment of the mentally ill. He was involved in much of the significant legislation listed below:

1833 No children under nine to work in a textile factory, hours restricted to 8 hrs for 9–11-year-olds and 12 hrs for 11–18-year-olds.
1841 Mines Act: no child under ten to work in a mine.
1842 System of apprenticeship abolished, Coal Mines Act stopped women and children under 13 working underground.
1847 No more than 10 hrs work a day for adults and children in mills and factories.
1868 Agricultural Gangs Act: no child under eight to be employed in a gang of farm workers.
1874 Factory Act: no child under ten to be employed in a factory.
1875 Climbing Boys Act: no boys to be sent up chimneys.

Starting Points	Main Activity	Simplified Activity	Extension Activity
V6 and **V7** *'Dr Bernardo (1) and (2)'* Explain that some people in Victorian times were very concerned about the poor and many worked to help improve their lives. Explain the 'evangelical' Christianity of Bernardo and Shaftesbury.	Explain that children have the same text but different missing information. They must not look at each other's text, but prepare to ask and answer questions. Pupils with the same sheet could do this preparation together and then change partners to ask the questions.	Give the children a copy of either sheet with the questions already written and the phrases containing the answers for their partner underlined. Read the complete text with them.	Ask the children to design a leaflet to raise money for one of Dr Bernardo's homes.
V8 *'Lord Shaftesbury'* Discuss with the children the different approaches to reform: the 'hands on' approach of Bernardo and the work to change legislation of Shaftesbury.	Tell children to read the text all the way through once before completing the sentences and comparing their choices with a partner.	Give the children a list of simple sentence beginnings (He believed in … He was president of … Employers were often cruel to children … and so on). Ask them to match them to the endings on the sheet.	Give the children suitable resources and ask them to find out some of the new laws in this period that improved conditions for children.

Plenary

Prepare a 'hot seat' activity: ask children to play Dr Bernardo and Lord Shaftesbury, and the rest to prepare a number of questions. Afterwards discuss as a class the way children's lives were changed by these two reformers.

Dr Bernardo (1)

Sheet for pupil A

● Read about Dr Bernardo, write questions to find out the missing information and prepare to answer questions from your partner.

Thomas Bernardo was born in _____ , in 1845. He went to St Patrick's Cathedral Grammar School. While he was there he saw boys being beaten and badly treated by the headmaster and this made him hate to see children abused. At the age of _____ he became a Christian, and from then on his religious beliefs were at the heart of everything he did.

He felt that God wanted him to be a medical missionary in China and he went to train as a doctor in London. While he was there the poverty and misery that he saw made him realise that this was where he should work. A young orphan called Jim Jarvis showed him _____ .
He found out that thousands of children slept on the streets and never went to school.

Bernardo dedicated his life to working with poor children. When he was only 23, and still a student at medical school, he opened a 'ragged' school in _____ .
The children learned to read and write, and they did practical work to help earn a living. The children still had nowhere to sleep and in 1871 he opened a home for boys, offering shelter, clothes, food and some work training. At first the number of boys was limited but one night a boy called 'Carrots', who had been turned away, died from _____ . After that Bernardo's homes never turned any child away.

He had great energy and determination. He raised money by producing magazines and leaflets, holding bazaars and giving speeches. His work sometimes got him into trouble with the law; he went to court for 'kidnapping' children from parents who were abusing them. Thomas Bernardo worked all his life to save children from poverty and hopelessness. When he died, in 1905, he had changed the lives of _____ children.

● Write the questions you are going to ask your partner.

_____

_____

_____

_____

_____

Dr Bernardo (2)

Sheet for pupil B

● Read about Dr Bernardo, write questions to find out the missing information and prepare to answer questions from your partner.

Thomas Bernardo was born in Dublin, Ireland, in _____ . He went to St Patrick's Cathedral Grammar School. While he was there he saw boys being beaten and badly treated by the headmaster and this made him hate to see children abused. At the age of 17 he became a Christian, and from then on his religious beliefs were at the heart of everything he did.

He felt that God wanted him to be a medical missionary in China and he went to train as a _____ in London. While he was there the poverty and misery that he saw made him realise that this was where he should work. A young orphan called Jim Jarvis showed him children sleeping on the roofs in the East End of London. He found out that thousands of children slept on the streets and never went to school.

Bernardo dedicated his life to working with poor children. When he was only 23, and still a student at medical school, he opened a 'ragged' school in Stepney (East London). The children learned to read and write, and they did practical work to help earn a living. The children still had nowhere to sleep and in _____ he opened a home for boys, offering shelter, clothes, food and some work training. At first the number of boys was limited but one night a boy called 'Carrots', who had been turned away, died from hunger and exposure. After that Bernardo's homes never turned any child away.

He had great energy and determination. He raised money by producing magazines and leaflets, holding bazaars and giving speeches. His work sometimes got him into trouble with the law; he went to court for _____ .
Thomas Bernardo worked all his life to save children from poverty and hopelessness. When he died, in _____ he had changed the lives of 60 000 children.

● Write the questions you are going to ask your partner.

_____

_____

_____

_____

_____

Lord Shaftesbury

- Read the text and use the sentence endings below to complete the unfinished sentences.

Christianity
worked to make life better for others
ordinary people
and beat them
an allotment to grow vegetables
houses built
at what age they could be employed
Ragged School Union
this affected him deeply

Anthony Ashley Cooper was born in 1801 in London. He was the eldest son of the sixth Earl of Shaftesbury. He went to boarding school at Harrow and then to Oxford University. In 1826 he entered parliament but instead of making a career for himself he always _____ .

He made a difference to the lives of thousands of children by his work to change the laws that said how many hours they could work, and _____
_____ . Also, he worked to abolish a system called 'apprenticeship', where children were under control of a master who often treated them cruelly _____ .

He visited hospitals in Lancashire and saw workers who had been disabled through accidents and _____ . He went into mines to gather evidence about the conditions that children worked under. He thought that children should have a free education and for 39 years he was chairman of the _____ . He believed that if people did not have good enough houses, they could not be healthy and he worked hard to get new _____ . On his own land, he built a model village where all the cottages had modern facilities (for the time) and _____ .

Like Dr Bernardo, he was a religious man who believed in _____ . Even though he was from a privileged background he always cared about the lives of _____ . He died in 1885.

Schools in Victorian Times

Learning Objectives

Children should:
- learn how universal education provision became established in Victorian times.
- know some ways in which schooling changed over the Victorian period.

Background

The first limited grants to education were in 1833. This was the first instance of acceptance by the government of responsibility for education of the poor. The grants were given to religious bodies to build charity schools or Sunday schools. 'Dame schools' were the name for schools run by one elderly lady carrying out a mixture of childcare and basic literacy. Workhouses and some factories had their own schools.

It is estimated that only 20 per cent of children in 1840 had any sort of schooling and most of them would be only attending Sunday school. From 1870, local councils were obliged to provide a primary school, run by a board of local dignitaries but, as they were not free, attendance (although compulsory) was usually poor. It was not until 1899 that a free primary education was available, 1902 for secondary.

Ragged schools were set up to cater for inner-city children who were not provided for by charity, church or dame schools. All kinds of buildings were converted and teachers, often working people themselves, delivered reading, writing, arithmetic and Bible study. They were attended by as many as 300 000 children during the 1840s, 1850s and 1860s. There were some clashes with school boards after 1870, and when free education was available they were no longer needed.

Starting Points	Main Activity	Simplified Activity	Extension Activity
V9 and **V10** *'Changes in Victorian schools (1) and (2)'* Explain that during Victorian times the number of children at school increased and the type of schools changed.	Explain that there are two pictures of schoolrooms, early and late Victorian, and that children should find out about each other's pictures by asking questions and describing them, not by looking!	Give the children a list of specific questions to ask and answer about the pictures. Are the children in rows? Have they all got books? Are they all the same age? And so on.	Ask the children to write about a day in each of the schoolrooms, from the child's point of view.
V11 *'The history of a ragged school: 46–48 Copperfield Road'* Recall what the children know about Dr Bernardo and explain what ragged schools were.	Ask for words to describe the building and the children in the picture. Explain how warehouses were used. Ask the children to read the text, discuss ideas with a partner and report to the class, before writing their own headlines and sentences.	Give the children a copy of the text with the appropriate sections underlined and ask them to write four headlines, but not the first sentences.	Give the children suitable resources and ask them to research the content of a lesson at a ragged school (or a school after 1870). Ask them to write the teacher's plan for the day.

Plenary

Ask the children what they would have to do to re-create a mid/late Victorian schoolroom in their own classroom. Make a list of changes. If possible, carry out the plan and hold a Victorian lesson, costume and strict discipline included!

Changes in Victorian schools (1)

Sheet for pupil A

● Study this picture and fill in the first column of the table with all the information you can.

● Find out from your partner about a schoolroom in late Victorian times and fill in the second column of the table.

	early Victorian schoolroom	late Victorian schoolroom
seating arrangement		
equipment		
ages of children		
number in class		
teacher		

Changes in Victorian schools (2)

Sheet for pupil B

● Study this picture and fill in the second column of the table with all the information you can.

● Find out from your partner about a schoolroom in early Victorian times and fill in the first part of the table.

	early Victorian schoolroom	late Victorian schoolroom
seating arrangement		
equipment		
ages of children		
number in class		
teacher		

The history of a ragged school: 46–48 Copperfield Road

1876 Dr Bernardo rented two warehouses to be used as a ragged school.
Each floor was made into a big classroom with a fireplace.
The warehouse doors were replaced with windows.
The basements were turned into playgrounds.

1877 The boys' and girls' infant schools were opened. The children received a free education, breakfast and dinner, and help to find their first job.

1879 The school became the largest ragged school in London.

1895 The classrooms had become so overcrowded that Dr Bernardo rented the warehouse next door and converted it in the same way.

1896 There were 1075 children attending the day school and 2460 attending the Sunday school.

1908 The school was shut down because the buildings were no longer suitable for a school. The children went to the local council schools, which now also cost nothing.

● Write a newspaper headline and a first sentence for the events in the history of the school.

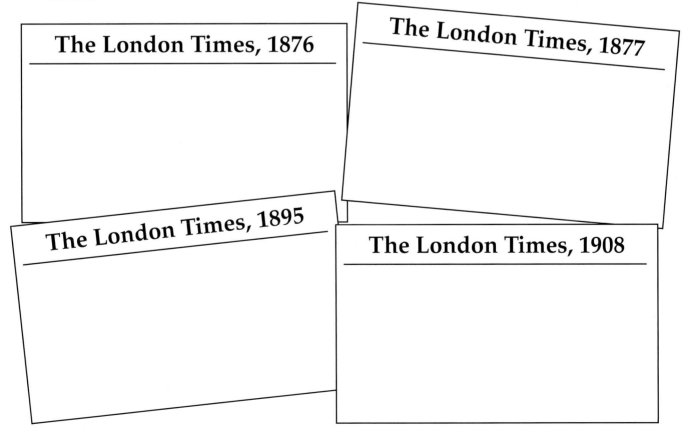

The London Times, 1876

The London Times, 1877

The London Times, 1895

The London Times, 1908

Games and Leisure

Learning Objectives

Children should:
- learn about games and leisure activities for Victorian children.
- understand that the type of leisure activities depended on family income.

Background

In wealthy families young children spent most of their time in the nursery, usually at the top of the house, looked after by a nanny. Their toys were mainly handmade, although, in late Victorian times, some toys were manufactured. On Sundays, the children would only be allowed to play games with a biblical theme. Although they had more time for play, wealthy children would probably have less company than poorer children, who met in the streets. In poorer families, children made their own toys and games; marbles were collected from drink bottle-tops; hoops were made by blacksmiths. With little traffic (and that only horse-drawn) the streets were safer than today.

The railways made a huge difference to sport and leisure. Railway companies were obliged to provide third-class carriages and to stop at every station, making a day at the seaside (on Bank Holidays, introduced in 1871) a possibility for working-class people. Seaside resorts boomed and traditions like fish and chips and donkey rides date from Victorian times. Also, for the first time, sports groups could travel to play other teams. The first FA (Football Association) cup final was in 1872 and the Football League began in 1888. Special trains took people to cricket matches and races.

It may be difficult for children today, who have many toys and have leisure facilities, to appreciate how entertaining a band, an organ grinder or a Punch and Judy show would be. Page 21 shows how children made their own entertainment, took on responsibility early, and were contented with little.

Starting Points	Main Activity	Simplified Activity	Extension Activity
V12 *'Children playing'* Explain that leisure time and games were different for wealthy and poor children.	Ask the children to study the pictures in pairs and to discuss answers to the questions. Ask individuals to report to the class before everyone writes their answers.	Ask the children to work with a partner (adult or child) who will help them with the oral descriptions and answers to the questions. Give them words and phrases to help them write the answers.	Give the children suitable resources and ask them to research other games played by Victorian children.
V13 *'A day of leisure'* Talk about the importance of the Church in Victorian times and how Sundays were a day of religious observance, rest and best clothes.	Discuss the games and entertainments, and ensure that children know what they are. Talk about mealtimes and what food they might eat. Ask children to write an outline plan before describing the day in detail.	Give the children a structured frame to help with a short piece of writing. After breakfast I … On the way I saw … I went home for my dinner. We had … and so on.	Give the children some resources that might be available to a Victorian child (wooden clothes peg, scraps of wood, brown paper, cotton fabric, wool, and so on). Ask them to make their own toy.
V14 *'Combining work and play'* Explain why washing took a long time in the Victorian era.	Read the text with the children and discuss it. Ask them to underline the words or phrases that will inform their picture, before starting to draw.	Begin as for the main activity. Give the children a copy of the text with the information to be included in the picture already underlined.	Ask the children to make a list of other ways in which Victorian children would probably be expected to help adults. Compare this with what they and their classmates do today.

Plenary

Compare leisure activities for Victorian children and children today by drawing a Venn diagram, where one circle represents children's leisure today and the other represents Victorian children's leisure.

Children playing

● Describe the two games shown in these pictures.

_____   _____

_____   _____

● Think about these questions and then write your answers.

Why did poorer children have less time to play? _____

Why were the streets safer than today? _____

Why did children make their own toys? _____

This picture shows wealthy Victorian children playing with a puppet show in their nursery. Their nanny is looking after them.

● Think about these questions and write your answers.

Why were wealthy children not allowed to play on Sundays?

_____

_____

_____

Would a wealthy child have more or less friends to play with than a poor child? Why?

_____

_____

A day of leisure

Imagine that you are living in late Victorian times and you belong to a working family. It is a Sunday, so you have some free time. Write a description of your day, choosing from the ideas below. Remember that many families went to church and children often went to Sunday school.

Street games

hopscotch
leapfrog
conkers
marbles
iron hoops

Evening games

Happy Families
snap
dominoes
charades

Entertainment

barrel organ

bandstand

Punch and Judy

Combining work and play

The writer of the text below, Mrs Layton, remembers how, as a child in the 1860s, she and her friends combined work and play. The text also explains why many children stayed away from school.

My fourth sister and I always stayed away from school on washing day to mind the babies. In the summer it was a real sport, because so many people did their washing on the same day, and everybody had large families and generally kept the elder girls, and sometimes boys, at home to mind the little ones. We used to plan to go out all together with our prams and babies into Victoria Park. Very few people had prams of their own, but could hire them at 1d [penny] an hour to hold one baby, or $1\frac{1}{2}$d an hour to hold two. Several mothers would pay a few pence for the hire of a pram and the children used to manage between them how they were used. I need hardly say each pram was used to its full seating capacity. The single pram had always to accommodate two and the double pram three or more, and we always kept them the full length of time for which we had paid. We would picnic on bread and treacle under the trees in the Park, and return home in the evenings a troop of happy but tired children.

● Use the information in this account to draw a picture of the children on a summer's day in the park.

Victorian Life

Learning Objectives

Children should:
- consider the way in which many aspects of life changed over this period.
- understand that children's futures were more subject to chance than they are today.

Background

By the time Queen Victoria's reign ended, young children were no longer working in mines and factories and a high percentage were attending school. Children were seen as scholars rather than wage earners. On the whole, their parents were better off: industry had created a larger middle class and provided jobs. The conditions and hours of working people had improved. There was a better understanding of the causes of disease; cities had underground sewers; and more city dwellers had access to clean water. There was also more of a belief in addressing the causes of crime than punishing the offender; the death penalty had been abolished for lesser crimes; prisoners were no longer transported. A police force existed to uphold the law. Also, by this time, only one fifth of the population was rural.

A poor underclass remained, scraping a living from casual work, often laid off, prone to disease and living in sub-standard housing. The chances of a Victorian child reaching a healthy and happy adulthood had improved over the years, but still depended on where they lived, and, to a much greater extent than today, the class they were born into. Life expectancy was still much lower. Although a basic education was available it was unlikely to provide them with an escape from their allotted place in the social order.

Starting Points	Main Activity	Simplified Activity	Extension Activity
V15 *'Changes over the Victorian era'* Recall how many aspects of life changed over the Victorian period.	Ask the children to discuss each of the aspects of life and how they changed, in pairs or small groups. Ask individuals to report back to the class before everyone completes the sheet.	Give the children simple sentences to copy or stick onto the table. (There were no laws to protect children. There were a lot of laws to protect children … and so on.)	Give the children access to more information about some of the changes and ask them to represent findings in the form of a diagram showing cause and effect. (What caused the changes? What was the result?) Use boxes and arrows.
V16 and **V17** *'Game of Chance' and 'Chance cards'* Discuss the way that the fate of Victorian children, especially in the early Victorian years, was much more dependent on chance than children's lives are today.	Photocopy page 26 onto thin card. Read and discuss the lucky and unlucky events that could befall a Victorian child, page 27. Discuss the fact that chimney sweeps are lucky and a downward-facing horseshoe is unlucky as it drops any good luck. Explain that the number of places to move forward or back should reflect the nature of the event. Provide thin card or thick paper to make the chance cards. Ask them to draw the lucky/unlucky symbol on the back of each card, sit in groups of four, and pool their cards for the game. If some events are repeated it doesn't matter; some will be more likely than others, like real life! To avoid one turn lasting too long, point out the rule that once a card has been taken, even if you land on another lucky/unlucky square, you don't take another card. To simplify the preparation activity for some children, give them events to sort into lucky/unlucky, and stick or copy on the back of the cards.		

Plenary

Ask the class to contribute page headings for a book about Victorian children. When you have a list of headings, ask them about pictures and information to include on each page.

Changes over the Victorian era

- Complete the table showing how things changed.

	early Victorian times	late Victorian times
laws		
school		
beliefs about childhood	*Children were expected to work. They had to be obedient and hardworking. They had no special rights.*	
transport		
wealth		*There were more middle-class people. Ordinary people had more money to spend.*
living conditions		
where they lived	*Most people lived in the countryside and worked on the land.*	

Game of Chance

3 Lucky Street

Place unlucky cards here

Place lucky cards here

START

Rules
1. Take it in turns to throw a die.
2. Move forward the correct number of squares.
3. If you land on a lucky/unlucky square, take a card and move forward or backward. If you land on another lucky/unlucky square, do not take another card.
4. The winner is the first person to reach the house.

FOLENS HISTORY IN ACTION 5

Chance cards

- Use this information to help you make chance cards for the game.

Ideas for unlucky events

Unlucky accidents could happen when ...
- families were crowded together sharing one building.
- buildings were dark and there was no electricity.
- all the water had to be carried up and down stairs.
- all the cooking was done on an open fire.

Illness was more common when ...
- the diet of poor people was mainly bread and butter, and potatoes. People didn't eat enough green vegetables and couldn't afford fruit.
- the family had only just enough money. If something extra was needed (a pair of shoes) the mother and children had less food.
- water was not clean.
- you had to pay the doctor and for medicine.

Money could easily run out when ...
- fathers decided how much of their wages to give to the mother for all the shopping.
- there were a lot of children in the family.
- the worst jobs were badly paid.
- workers were laid off.
- there was no unemployment benefit.
- there was no sick pay.

Ideas for lucky events

Somebody in the family ...
- got a job.
- got a better paid job.
- was given a gift.
- found a better place to live.

A wealthier friend or relation ...
- sent some money.
- offered to take some of the children into their house.
- paid for schooling.

The local council ...
- provided clean water.
- installed a sewerage system in the street.
- provided better housing.
- opened a school nearby, with no charge for education.
- rented plots of land (allotments) for people to grow vegetables.

Sources of Information

Learning Objectives

Children should:
- learn about sources of information for researching the local area.
- find evidence of changes in Victorian times in the local area from a comparison of census returns or other sources.

Background

Information from the census, a government questionnaire, has been collected every ten years since 1801. The information is made public after 100 years, although the original returns for before 1841 were not kept. The 1841 census does not give the exact address or place of birth. It lists the head of household first but does not give the relationship to the other occupants of the house.

Census returns from 1841 to 1901, Ordnance Survey maps and street or trade directories can be found at local Record Offices (no charge but appointment needed) or local libraries. The 1901 census is available on the Internet. School logbooks are sometimes held at schools but more usually at the local Record Office or Education Office. Most libraries have a local history section with collections of photographs and books by local historians. Other visual records can sometimes be found in antique shops and personal collections. Photography began in the 1840s but photographs of the later Victorian period (from 1870) are much easier to find.

Starting Points	Main Activity	Simplified Activity	Extension Activity
L1 *'Finding information'* Talk about sources of information for historical research, show some examples and discuss where to obtain information from.	Ask the children to make a record of the discussion by completing the table. Allow them to confer with partners.	Give the children a list of the words and phrases needed to complete the table and ask them to stick or copy them in the right place.	Ask the children to compile a list of questions that they would like to find answers to in researching their local area.
L2 *'1841 and 1891 census'* Talk in more detail about census returns. Have copies of the 1841 and 1891 returns for the area around the school available. Select the streets you want the children to use for the comparison table.	Ask children to study the two examples closely and find out how the information gathered is different. Ask individuals to report and discuss possible reasons for the changes. Give out copies of the census area children are to study to enable them to complete the table.	Begin as for the main activity but ask children to highlight or underline the differences on the 1891 census, rather than write a full answer. Ask them to count the number of adults and children (ages above and below 18). This information can be added to data collected by the rest of the class.	Give the children dictionaries and ask them to look up the meaning of occupations that are no longer known or common. Occupations from the census could also be classified, for example agricultural/industrial/ services. Ask them to report to the class.
L3 *'Changes in Britain'* Recall the changes in Victorian times from the previous unit (page 25). Discuss how this relates to your local area and which sources provide evidence.	Either use the results of the comparison of census returns on page 30 or provide children with sources that give evidence of change in the area. Give them one example to begin the table.	Ask the children to work with a partner who will read the text with them. Give the children a table with some of the evidence filled in and ask them to conclude what the change was and write a sentence explaining it.	Give the children access to suitable sources and ask them to record changes for which there are two pieces of evidence. For example, fewer children died. Evidence: more children per adult in census; fewer deaths recorded in school logbook.

Plenary

Ask the children to prepare a radio programme giving advice to children about how to research their local area. Some of the class could prepare a script about sources; while others rehearse an interview about the work they have done themselves so far. Record the programme.

Finding information

● Complete the table.

source	where to get it from	type of information
census ![census image]	*local Record Office or library*	*names, ages, sex, occupation, birthplace of each member of a household*
local maps ![map image]		
photographs and postcards ![postcard image]		
paintings and sketches ![sketch image]		
school logbook ![logbook image]		
street directory ![directory image]		

1841 and 1891 census

1841

Village or house	Name	Age and sex	Profession, trade, employment or independent means	Born in same county?
Stoke Row	William Giles	61/m	Carpenter and builder	Yes

1891

Schedule no. and village or house name	Name	Relation to head	Condition	Age and sex	Rank, profession or occupation	Where born
Grocer's shop	William James Taylor	Head	Married	30 M	Grocer, draper and baker	Caversham, Oxon
	Julia Taylor	Wife	Married	29 F		Ipsden, Oxon

- The 1891 census gives more information. What is the extra information it gives?

_____

_____

- Complete this table for your local area census.

data field		1841	1891
Number of households			
Number of	males		
	females	+	+
	Total	=	=
Number of people born outside area			
Most popular occupations			

Changes in Britain

● Choose the correct words in this text.

> The Victorian years were a time of **slow/rapid** change in Britain. Many factories and mills were built. Thousands of people left the countryside to work in the towns and cities. Cities became **more/less** crowded. There were **more/less** jobs in factories, railways, building, and services like shops, pubs, cleaning and washing. There were **more/less** jobs in farming.
>
> The total population of the country grew **bigger/smaller**. People in 1891 usually lived **shorter/longer** lives than people in 1841. **More/less** children lived past their fifth birthday in 1891. This meant that, on average, families were **smaller/bigger**. More houses were needed because there were **more/less** families.

● Can you see any evidence of these changes in your local area? Use the census return or other sources to complete the table.

Change	Evidence

The Effects of Victorian Railways

Learning Objectives

Children should:
- appreciate the impact of the railways on Victorian society.
- understand why there was opposition to the railways.
- apply knowledge of the effects of the railways to research of the local area.

Background

The railways boom impacted strongly on Victorian society. Between 1820 and 1850, 6000 miles of railways were put into operation. They reached the remotest areas of the countryside and the city centres. The country was networked together in a new way. Minutes were now marked on time pieces and the time across the country had to be synchronised. The speed of movement was totally transformed. Day trips for the working classes were possible for the first time; sports matches could be played against teams from other cities. Cheap transport boosted industry and made goods cheaper. The railways and industry became the biggest employers. The canals declined but coaches had more work taking people to and from the stations.

There were negative effects. Huge engineering works were involved in order to make the line flat. Decrepit housing in city centres was often demolished to lay tracks, without providing an alternative for the inhabitants. Heritage buildings were threatened and sometimes destroyed. In the rush to make money, and lack of a national plan, too many lines were built. Accidents were frequent. The first phase of opposition (1825–44) was universal and local petitions were formed against every new line. Small towns often succeeded in getting stations located outside of the centre. After 1850, when most lines had been laid, protest was more about finance and organisation.

Starting Points	Main Activity	Simplified Activity	Extension Activity
L4 *'Effects of the railways'* Explain how rapidly the railways expanded and talk about the effects on people's lives.	Ask the children to look at the captions and pictures in pairs and use them to record the effects discussed, using a separate sheet.	Give the children a list of words or phrases that they can match to each picture.	Ask the children to make a list of evidence of the changes we might find today, and where we would find them.
L5 *'Opposition to the railways'* Talk about the reaction of people at the time to the expansion of the railways.	Ask children to read the text and discuss it in pairs, before reporting to the class and recording answers. Ask them to cut out the bubbles and work in pairs or groups to sort them into two piles.	Ask the children to do the second activity only. Ask them to work with a partner who will read the speech bubbles with them and encourage them to discuss.	Ask the children to write a letter to a newspaper, as a Victorian, either agreeing or disagreeing with the fears expressed in the bubbles.
L6 *'Your local area and the railways'* Tell the children when your nearest railway was built, look at maps of before and after. Teach them the Ordnance Survey (OS) symbols for cutting, embankment and so on.	Read the first column with the class. (Alter to make it more specific to your area.) Ask them to work down the second column in pairs and discuss. Either provide sources for research or arrange to carry it out on another day.	Ask the children to work with a partner who will help them to reread the first column and complete the second. Give them a shorter list of items for research, using only one or two sources.	Ask the children to produce their own local history pamphlet about the coming of the railways in your area, using the information they have gathered.

Plenary

Organise a debate, with the children playing Victorians of the local area in 1850, some in favour of the railways and some against.

Effects of the railways

● Explain how each of these things was affected by the expansion of the railways in Victorian times.

landscape	time	environment
city centres and inhabitants	leisure	sport
jobs	price of goods	canals

Opposition to the railways

- Read these two pieces of evidence and list the problems.

Letter in a newspaper

On the line of this railway I have built a comfortable house with a good view of the countryside. Now, imagine how I feel when, sitting at breakfast with my family, enjoying the pure air, my house is suddenly filled with dense smoke of stinking gas, my table covered with dirt, and the features of my wife and family almost invisible. Nothing can be heard except clanking iron, and the rude songs or swearing of the drivers of these infernal machines.

Deaths and injuries in rail accidents

January–June 1852
113 killed, 264 injured

January–June 1853
148 killed, 191 injured

_____

_____

_____

Here are some of the reasons that people in Victorian times opposed the railways. Decide which fears were justified (turned out to be right) and which were not.

The natural beauty of the landscape will be ruined.

Important historical buildings will be knocked down.

The behaviour of farm animals may be affected. Hens might not lay eggs; cows might not graze near railways.

Cuttings and embankments will collapse, taking houses and people with them.

Some people will lose their jobs, for example canal workers, coach drivers, inn-keepers on the roads.

Too many railway lines are being built because people want to make money.

FOLENS HISTORY IN ACTION 5 © Folens (copiable page)

Your local area and the railways

- Complete the first column, and then carry out your research and complete as much of the second column as possible.

possible changes/effects	possible sources of information (for example, maps, census, trade directories, photographs, local history books)	evidence found

landscape: cuttings built
   embankments built
   bridge built
   tunnel built
   buildings demolished		

canal use declined		
a local industry (factory) grew bigger		
a local industry began		
new jobs were created		
new roads or streets were given names related to the railway		
people took trips to the seaside or a nearby city		
there were sports matches with teams from other towns/cities		
people protested (small towns often protested against having the station in the town centre and it was built outside the town)		

Finding Evidence of Victorian Times

Learning Objectives

Children should:
- know the main features of Victorian buildings.
- be able to identify other forms of evidence of Victorian times in the local area.

Background

Victorian houses were mostly built of brick with slate roofs. Workers' terraced houses are still used in towns today, the outside 'privy' and coalhouse gone, a bathroom added upstairs. Larger and later houses tend to have more decorative features. Many schools were built around 1870, and many churches were rebuilt or altered.

There were a number of influences on Victorian architecture; 'Gothic Revival' was one of the strongest. The inspiration was medieval: arches, pointed windows and features from medieval cathedrals. The Palace of Westminster is built in this style, as were many important civic buildings.

Fortunately for us, the Victorians created parks and gardens in cities and towns. They collected specimens from all over the world and established botanical gardens and greenhouses. The mature plane trees, cherry trees, horse chestnuts, poplars and so on, that line city streets now, were planted in Victorian times.

Starting Points	Main Activity	Simplified Activity	Extension Activity
L7 *'Identifying Victorian houses'* Look at photographs of Victorian houses and identify features. Introduce the architectural vocabulary needed for the activity.	Allow time for children to label the features. Discuss the persuasive language used by estate agents before asking them to complete the advertisement.	After the children have labelled the features, ask them to write a description of a Victorian house, using the words as appropriate.	Give the children suitable resources and ask them to research the different types of houses Victorians lived in: villas (large detached), tied cottages, workhouses. Ask them to report their findings to the class.
L8 *'Victorian civic buildings and parks'* Talk about the pride that many Victorians felt in their cities and their country, and the way that buildings and parks reflected this feeling.	Read the information with the class and explain new vocabulary. Read an example of a Victorian news report and discuss features of style before asking children to write their own report.	Give the children a photograph of either the town hall or the park. Ask them to imagine visiting it for the first time, and write a letter to a friend describing what they saw.	Give the children a photograph of a Victorian Town Hall (or similar), and ask them to compare architectural features using a photograph of a pre-Victorian (Georgian) building.
L9 *'Evidence of Victorian times'* Plan a walk round the local area to take in as much evidence of Victorian times as possible.	Go through the evidence listed and make sure that children understand what to look for. Use the sheet either to make notes during the walk, or to write up notes back in the classroom.	Give the children a copy of the sheet with questions specific to the local area written in the boxes (What is the date over the door of the building? What shape are the church windows? And so on.)	Ask the children to develop their notes into a 'history walk' leaflet, with map, numbered points, and descriptions of Victorian features.

Plenary

Tell the children about 'Blue Badge' history tour guides. The 'Blue Badge' is awarded to people who undertake a programme of training, assignments and written exams in the history of their local area, and British history and culture. They learn the professional techniques of the tour guide and can register and offer their services locally. Ask them to prepare a test (a list of questions), which a person would have to pass before qualifying to lead a guided tour about Victorian times in their local area.

Identifying Victorian houses

● Label the pictures with these words to describe architectural features.

For workers' houses – brick walls, slate roof, outside toilet, rows of houses built 'back-to-back'.

For larger houses – steps to the front door, bay window, sash window, gable on roof, barge boards (on the edge of the roof), Flemish brick bonding (a way of laying the bricks)

● Use a Victorian house you know, or a photograph, to write an estate agent's advert.

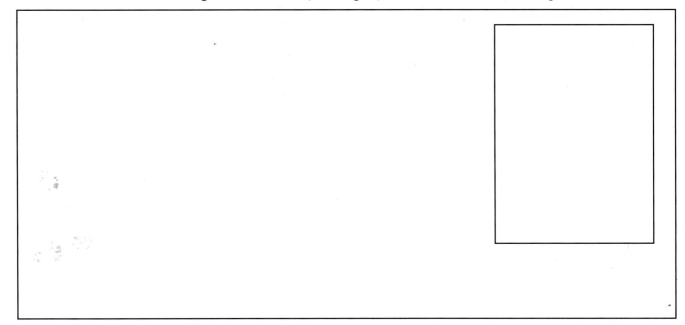

Victorian civic buildings and parks

● Read the information given below. Choose one and write a Victorian newspaper report about the opening.

Manchester Town Hall

Year completed: 1887

Architect: Alfred Waterhouse

Purpose: administrative centre, to show that Manchester was an important city

Special features: decorated with bees, symbol of Manchester's industry

Location: Albert Square, central Manchester

Architectural style: neo-Gothic

The Palm House at Kew Gardens

Year completed: 1848 (begun 1844)

Designer: Richard Turner

Purpose: to create a warm, humid environment to grow tropical plants

Special features: open span without pillars, 50 ft (15.2 m) wide; technology from ship building used, design is like an upturned ship's hull; 12 boilers underneath to heat it

Location: Kew Gardens, London

The London Times, 18 ___

_____

_____

_____

_____

_____

_____

_____

Evidence of Victorian times

● Use this sheet to record all the evidence that remains of Victorian times in your local area.

Common evidence of Victorian times	Description of evidence in our local area
civic buildings	
churches	
schools	
parks and gardens	
houses	
mature trees in street (over 100 years old)	
names of streets, squares, parks	
other	

Britain Since 1948

Learning Objectives

Children should:
- be able to describe some changes in communications, transport and energy supply since 1948.
- appreciate differences in the information obtained from a range of primary and secondary sources.

Background

In the 1950s letters and telephone were the most common ways to communicate; hand-delivered telegrams were used for urgent messages. In the 1970s fax and telex machines were also available. By the 1990s answer machines were common, email was widely used and the mobile phone boom had begun. Telegrams became redundant. Communication is now cheaper and faster and has contributed to the creation of the 'global village'; distances have become less significant.

The M1 was opened in 1959 in a spirit of optimism, now replaced with traffic jams and road rage. Railways were allowed to close or deteriorate, while the road building programme led to the discovery that as more roads were built traffic figures grew. Car ownership has soared and led to the demise of town centres as people drive to supermarkets and travel greater distances between home and work.

Like the car and the motorway, nuclear energy was seen as the beginning of a new era; nine more stations were built in the decade following Calderhall, supplying a quarter of our electricity. The problem of the disposal of nuclear waste, the potential damage to the environment, the accidents at Three Mile Island (USA) and Chernobyl, the connection with nuclear weapons (the Windscale/Sellafield plant was also intended to make weapons-grade plutonium) all contributed to the change of attitude. The current programme is to close the oldest reactors and invest in alternatives, like wind, solar and wave power.

Starting Points	Main Activity	Simplified Activity	Extension Activity
B1 *'Communications'* Talk about the way that the children and their families send short- and long-distance messages today.	Ask the children to discuss, in pairs, the availability, speed and cost of sending messages since 1950 before asking them to record their answers.	Begin as for the main activity and ask children to complete the table. Omit the two questions from their copy of the sheet; ask them to write a sentence to say whether it is easier or more difficult to send messages today.	Ask the children to research satellites and find out how they have changed communications.
B2 *'Road travel'* Discuss the advantages and disadvantages of road travel today. Explain that cars were too expensive for most people before the 1950s.	Ask the children to study and discuss the information given in pairs. Ask them to write a report on road travel on a separate sheet.	Ask the children to work with a partner who will read and discuss the sources with them. Give them a list of questions to answer about the information (When did the M1 open? Are there more or less cars? And so on).	Ask the children to list the different types of source (photograph, table, quote, and map) and to describe the difference in the information given.
B3 *'Nuclear power'* Tell children about the different ways electricity is generated. Discuss the advantages and disadvantages of nuclear energy. Talk about forms of clean energy.	Look at the information from each source with the class. Discuss the difference in information from photograph/quote/headline. Ask the children to complete the sheet individually or in pairs.	Begin as for the main activity. Give the children sentences to complete to fill in the reasons for protesting. Give them words to remind them of the alternative forms of energy.	Ask the children to carry out a survey of the attitude of adults in the school to nuclear energy and to compare this with the quote on page 43.

Plenary

Generate two lists: other changes in technology to research, and sources of information. Ask individuals to pick a topic and say what type of information they might get from photographs/newspapers/tables/graphs/and so on.

Communications

- Label these ways of sending messages.

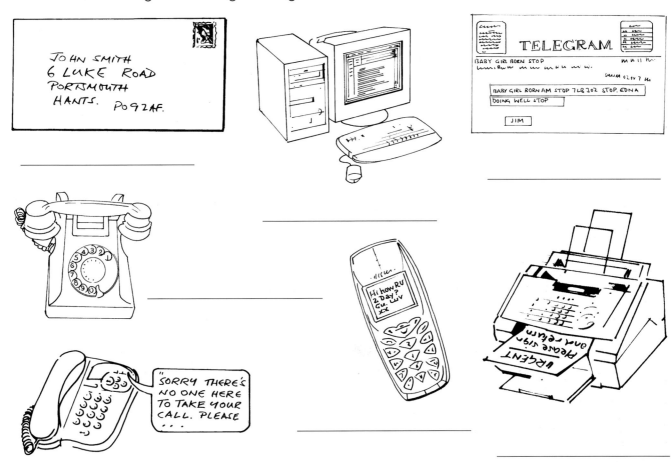

JOHN SMITH
6 LUKE ROAD
PORTSMOUTH
HANTS.   PO 9 2AF.

TELEGRAM

BABY GIRL BORN STOP

BABY GIRL BORN AM STOP 7LB 3OZ STOP. EDNA
DOING WELL STOP

JIM

"SORRY THERE'S NO ONE HERE TO TAKE YOUR CALL. PLEASE ..."

Hi how R U
2 Day?
Gu. Luv
XX

URGENT
Please sign
and return

_____   _____   _____

_____   _____

_____

- Draw or write the methods available for each year.

1950s	
1970s	
today	

- Describe what has happened to the speed and cost of sending a message.

_____

_____

- How has this changed people's lives?

_____

_____

Road travel

- Explain what these sources tell us about road travel since 1948.

Drawing of the media at the opening of the M1, 1959

… magnificent motorway opening up a new era in road travel, in keeping with the new, exciting, scientific age in which we live.

Quote from Ernest Marples, Minister of Transport, 2 November 1959

Traffic comparison chart

Number of vehicles on M1 per day	
1959	13 000
2002	88 000

Drawing of traffic jam, 2005

Map of UK motorway network – 1960	Map of UK motorway network – 2000
	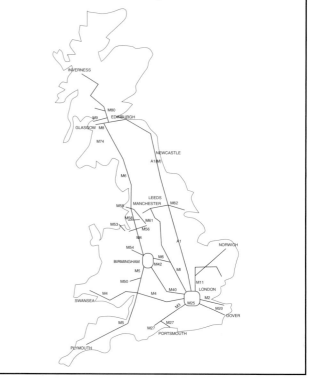

Nuclear power

- Look at these sources.

Headline, 17 October 1956

QUEEN OPENS FIRST NUCLEAR POWER PLANT

It may be that after 1965 every new power station being built will be an atomic power station.

Quote from Richard Butler, Lord Privy Seal, 17 October 1965

- What did people think about nuclear power in the 1960s?

_____

_____

_____

_____

_____

- What reasons did people have for protesting? Clues: waste, accidents, weapons.

_____

_____

_____

_____

- Draw pictures to represent alternative clean forms of energy being trialled today.

Changes at Work

Learning Objectives

Children should:
- be able to describe some of the changes in the world of work.
- be able to use a variety of sources to obtain information.

Background

The years since 1948 have seen the decline of traditional industries like steel works, shipyards and coal mining, and the increase of service industries and businesses based on the microchip. This means that there are less unskilled or semi-skilled manual jobs and more professional, managerial and technical jobs. Far more women go out to work.

The increase in the number of computers based on the microchip has been exponential, increasing the speed of communication, and the storage and retrieval of information. Some jobs have become redundant, but others have been created. The figures given in the table on page 46 are simplified; the range and price of available computers obviously varied, but the overall trend is clear.

The miners' strike of 1972 impacted heavily on the country; it lasted for seven weeks and led to power cuts and the declaration of a state of emergency. Whereas this strike was about pay, the 1980s miners' strike was about pit closures and was not successful. Where communities were based round traditional industries the effect of their decline was devastating.

Starting Points	Main Activity	Simplified Activity	Extension Activity
B4 *'Occupations'* Explain the way that job types are categorised for the collection of data. Give some examples of the types of graph used on page 45.	Ask the children to work through the tasks orally in pairs. Ask individuals to report on their discussion before everyone completes the sheet.	Give the children a copy of the sheet, with sentences partly written to explain the graphs. Make sure that they understand the graphs and ask them to complete the sentences.	Ask the children to find out the main employers in their local area in 1948 and the main employers now. If possible, arrange a visit from a local employer to talk about the jobs that people do.
B5 *'Computers and the office'* Talk about how computers are used in the work place, and how some of these jobs were done before computers.	Allow time for children to study and discuss the table and photograph in pairs or small groups. Ask some individuals to express the conclusions that can be drawn from the table before everyone completes the sheet.	Give the children a copy of the sheet with questions for the table: What has happened to the price of computers?... the number... and so on.	Give the children a list of jobs and ask them to describe how each of these people would use a computer at work. If possible arrange for a visitor to explain how their job has changed with the introduction of computers.
B6 *'Miners' strikes, 1972 and 1985'* Explain the importance of traditional industries after the war. Discuss the nature of the different sources: factual/emotive/ how memorable/strength of impact.	Ask children to study the information and find out what happened to the coal mining industry. Ask some individuals to report on the effect of the different sources before everyone completes the task.	Ask the children to cut out the four sources, stick them on a blank sheet and write a sentence for each, saying the main message that it gives.	Ask the children to prepare a list of questions for an enquiry into other traditional industries, or changes in work, since 1948.

Plenary

Ask the children to make statements to summarise the changes in working life since 1948. Generate a list of further questions and discuss the type of sources that would supply the answers.

Occupations

- Label the types of work above using the words from the key.

Key
- ☐ Professional
- ◼ (grey) Managerial and technical
- ⬚ Skilled
- ■ Partly skilled
- ▨ Unskilled

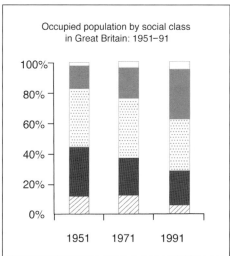

Occupied population by social class in Great Britain: 1951–91

100%
80%
60%
40%
20%
0%

1951 1971 1991

- What does this bar graph tell us about the number of people doing each type of job since 1951?

_____

_____

_____

_____

_____

_____

- What does this graph tell us about unemployment since 1948?

_____

_____

_____

_____

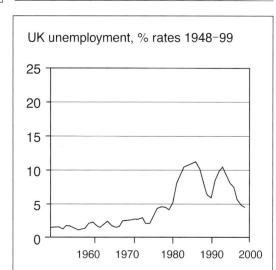

UK unemployment, % rates 1948–99

25
20
15
10
5
0

1960 1970 1980 1990 2000

Computers and the office

● Study the table and explain how the price, size and number of computers have changed.

year	no. of computers	size	price £
1950s	250+	filled a large room	£500 000
1960s	20 000	size of a large cupboard	£70 000
1980s	30 million	fitted on a desk	£10 800+
2005	350 million	fitted in a backpack	£600+

_____

_____

_____

_____

_____

_____

_____

_____

_____

_____

_____

_____

_____

_____

● Look at this photograph of an office in the early 1950s. Draw what it might look like today on a separate piece of paper.

Miners' strikes, 1972 and 1985

Miners marching through London in 1972

TV News report in 1972

Miners now into the sixth week of their strike over pay have been picketing power stations and all other sources of fuel supply in an attempt to step up pressure on the government.

From today, electricity will be switched off on a rota basis between 07:00 and 24:00 every day. It means consumers will face longer power cuts, up from six to nine hours.

• Explain the different type of information we get about the strike from each of these sources.

_____

_____

_____

_____

_____

_____

_____

_____

_____

_____

WHEN THEY CLOSE A PIT

THEY KILL A COMMUNITY

Poster, 1985

• Use the line graph to explain what has happened to the mining industry since 1948.

_____

_____

_____

_____

Coal production in the UK: 1900–99

Tons (millions)

350

300

250

200

150

100

50

0

1950   1960   1970   1980   1990

FOLENS HISTORY IN ACTION 5

Changes in Population

Learning Objectives

Children should:
- understand that immigration from Commonwealth countries has been a significant social change in post-war Britain.
- be able to describe some of the ways that society has changed as a result of immigration.

Background

The arrival of a ship called the *Empire Windrush* from the Caribbean in 1948 is the symbol of the beginning of large-scale immigration to the UK. Over the twentieth century, as a whole, immigration has been balanced by emigration from Britain. In the first half of the century there was a large exodus to the colonies. After the immigration of the forties, fifties and sixties, there was a period of greater migration in the seventies and eighties; thousands of families went to Australia, New Zealand and South Africa. In the nineties immigration was high again, but between 1901 and 1997 there was a net loss of 15 600 000 people.

Racism was a fact of life in the 1950s. Signs in houses with rooms to let, stating: 'no blacks, no Irish, no children, no dogs' were common. Stronger sentiments were expressed by groups from far right and fascist organisations. Black and Asian settlers had to deal with racial prejudice in finding jobs and accommodation. Race Relations Acts in 1965, 1968, 1976 and 2000 have helped to improve racial equality. Violence has been relatively rare and confined to poor areas where white and black communities are competing for jobs and housing. While there is still progress to be made to achieve true equality of opportunity, many British cities have benefited in terms of cultural diversity.

Starting Points	Main Activity	Simplified Activity	Extension Activity
B7 *'New settlers in Britain'* Talk about settlement in Britain before 1948: Romans, Anglo-Saxons, Vikings, Normans, Irish (1800s). Look at a map and recall where these settlers came from.	Ask the children, either individually or in pairs, to read the text and, with the help of an atlas, mark the the places the settlers came from. Discuss children's own knowledge of immigrant groups, especially those that may have been omitted from the text.	Ask the children to work with a partner who will read the text with them and help them to find the relevant countries on the map.	Ask the children to find out, through reading or interviews, the range of reasons that immigrants had for immigrating, and to report their findings to the class.
B8 *'Personal stories'* Talk about the difficulties experienced by the immigrant communities.	Read the texts with the children and discuss some of the issues raised before asking them to complete the table on a separate sheet.	Give the children sentences about Lajpat and Leroy and ask them to sort the sentences into successes or difficulties and use them to create a table.	Ask the children to research, by reading or interview, more stories to add to their table.
B9 *'The effects of new settlers'* Talk about the way society has been enriched by different ethnic groups, drawing on the children's own experience where possible.	Ask the children to write (or illustrate) all the examples they can think of enrichment. Allow them to exchange ideas or ask individuals to contribute interesting examples.	If children's knowledge and experience is limited, give them a range of examples and ask them to stick or copy them into the appropriate box.	Ask the children to choose one of the categories to research in more detail and provide suitable resources.

Plenary

Work with the class on a plan to present the material they have collected as a radio programme about migration. Include introductions and features such as personal stories and interviews.

New Settlers in Britain

- Read the text and use an atlas to mark the places the settlers came from on the map. Label the map with the names of the countries.

In the nineteenth and twentieth centuries Britain took control of countries all over the world, including India, parts of Africa, and the Caribbean. The taxes these countries paid, and the cheap materials they supplied, helped to make Britain a wealthy country. After the Second World War, many countries, including India and many in Africa, became independent but were members of the 'British Commonwealth'. When Britain needed more workers after the Second World War the government put advertisements in newspapers inviting people to come and live in Britain.

Many European immigrants were from Germany, Poland, the old Soviet Union (now separate countries like Lithuania, Latvia and Estonia), Hungary, Italy and Ireland. In the 1950s there were large numbers of settlers from the Commonwealth countries, particularly Jamaica in the Caribbean, India (Gujarat region), and Pakistan (East Pakistan later became Bangladesh). The new communities were mostly in cities and brought a variety of different customs, food, dress, languages, music and religions; this was an important change in British society.

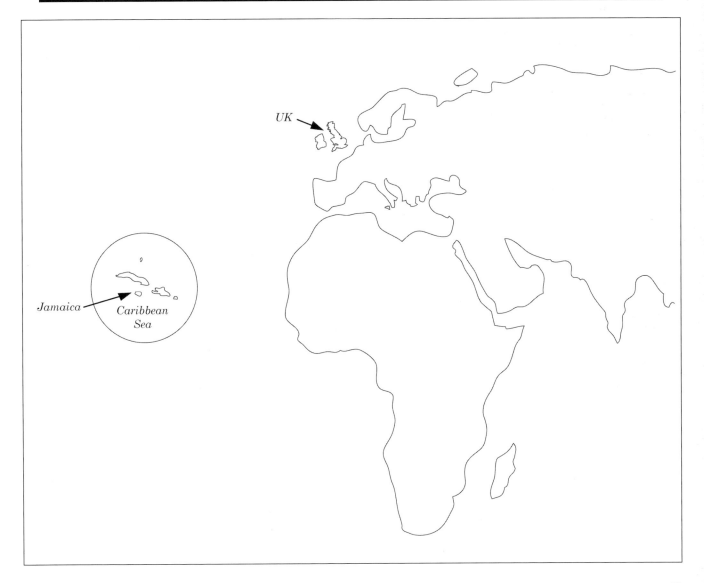

Personal stories

INSPECTOR LOGAN – WORKING TO IMPROVE RACE RELATIONS IN BRITAIN

Lajpat Rai Vij

Lajpat Rai Vij was born in 1924 in Taiwan. He came to England in 1947 when he was 23 years old, and stayed with his Uncle Salgram in Laurel Road, Liverpool.

At first Lajpat could only find work going from door to door, selling women's clothes. He sent money to his family back home so that his wife and young daughter could make the journey to Liverpool. He bought a shoe shop in Rainhill in 1955 but by the early 1960s changed the premises into a supermarket. Lajpat also opened a toy and fancy goods warehouse in Islington, Liverpool.

Lajpat was one of the first Indians to own his own home and he offered support to his fellow settlers. He played an important role in the local Indian community and was the first President of the Hindu Cultural Organisation in Liverpool. Lajpat died in 1977, aged 52.

When Leroy Logan's father was badly assaulted by the police in 1982 he realised that he could either become anti-police or become a policeman and work on the inside to reduce the possibility of this happening to anyone again.

Now, as a Chief Inspector with more than 20 years experience with the Metropolitan Police, he has received a number of awards for his work to develop anti-racist policies and build community and race relations.

He was born in London, but spent his early years in Jamaica, where his primary school was strict. 'I miss the discipline; I found that it was really inspiring. A lot of chatter that I could get away with in London I couldn't get away with in Jamaica.'

He returned to London but found that teachers did not encourage him. 'I was told by the teachers that I could not aspire to what I wanted to be, because I wanted to be a doctor but they said "No you could never be a doctor". That really traumatised me and my father went to the teacher and told him, 'Don't ever tell my son that he can't be whatever he wanted to be.' I have held onto that drive that I learned when I was in Jamaica and it has been with me ever since.'

- Read these stories and create a table. Add other stories to the table as you learn about them.

Name	Successes	Difficulties
Lajpat Rai Vij	bought his own shop	

The effects of new settlers

● Describe how life in Britain has changed as a result of the new communities.

Food	Languages	Clothes and fashion
	كيارى بنانا	

Laws/race relations	Music/entertainment	Other

Comparing the Decades

Learning Objectives

> **Children should:**
> - be able to sequence important events and movements in society between 1950 and today by decade.
> - collect and present information from a variety of sources.

Background

> For the first time, teenagers in the fifties stopped dressing like their parents, had their own money to spend and their own music. This was the rock and roll era. 'Teddy boys' were one of the first teenage cults. In the early sixties there were opposing gangs of Mods and Rockers. Hippies believed in love and peace and used hallucagenic drugs. Skinheads appeared in the late sixties. Punk was the outstanding movement of the seventies (body piercing with safety pins, dustbin bags as clothing). Heavy metal and reggae were also popular forms of music. In the late seventies and early eighties there was a New Romantic phase of flamboyant clothing. In the late eighties 'house' music was popular, as were 'raves' held at large venues out in the country, and the drug 'ecstasy'. In the nineties, British born Asians popularised 'Banghra' music and Manchester bands Blur and Oasis dominated mainstream popular music.
>
> The dates for the events in the news are:
>
> Coronation of Elizabeth II, 2 June 1953
> Roger Bannister runs a mile in under four minutes, 6 May 1954
> England wins the football World Cup, 30 July 1966
> First landing on the moon, 20 July 1969
> Decimal day, 15 February 1971
> First 'test tube' baby born, 25 July 1978
> Wedding of Prince Charles and Lady Diana, 29 July 1981
> Greenham Common protest, 1983–88
> Manchester bomb, 15 June 1996
> Death of Diana, Princess of Wales, 31 August 1997

Starting Points	Main Activity	Simplified Activity	Extension Activity
B10, **B11** and **B12** *'Music', 'Fashion'* and *'Events in the news'*	The activities on pages 53–55 can be used either as a starting point for the creation of posters for each decade, or for posters on one of the three topics. For decade posters, seat the children in groups of five, each child allocated to one decade. Ask them to discuss and sort the pictures from all three activities so that each child has three pictures to use as a starting point for their own decade poster.		
	Alternatively, ask the children to sequence the pictures for each topic and choose one topic for further research, such as creating a poster about music, fashion or important events for the whole period, displayed by decade.		
	In either case, the pictures are a starting point for discussion and display, with children carrying out their own enquiry to complete the poster on thin card or paper of A3 or A2 size.		

Plenary

> Ask individual children to report on the decade or topic they have investigated.

Music

- Sequence these pictures into decades, from the fifties to the nineties. Use them as a starting point for a poster about one decade, or about music from 1950 to the present day.

The Smiths

Live Aid

Blur and Oasis

The Clash

Elvis Presley

Bob Marley

The Beatles

Sukhbir, the 'Prince of Banghra'

Bill Haley and the Comets

Fashion

- Label each picture with a decade from the fifties to the nineties. Use them as a starting point for a poster about one decade, or about fashion from 1950 to 2000.

FOLENS HISTORY IN ACTION 5

Events in the news

● Sequence these pictures into decades, from the fifties to the nineties. Use them as a starting point for a poster about one decade, or about events in the news from 1950 to 2000.

First 'test-tube' baby

Roger Bannister runs a mile in under four minutes

Manchester bomb

First landing on the moon

Decimal day

England wins the football World Cup

Coronation of Elizabeth II

Death of Diana, Princess of Wales

Wedding of Prince Charles and Lady Diana

Greenham Common protest

Changes at Home

Learning Objectives

Children should:
- be able to describe some changes in home life since 1948.
- appreciate how these changes have influenced their own lives today.

Background

In the 1950s people (usually women) shopped in town centres or at groups of suburban local shops. They carried a shopping basket to the baker, butcher, grocer and greengrocer and left babies outside in prams! The first supermarkets were in town centres, often rebuilt after bomb damage in the war. Car ownership became more widespread during the sixties and by the eighties most people were driving to large new supermarkets with car parks, often located away from town centres. Local shops have been hardest hit; thousands have closed down. There was a housing shortage after the war and new estates were designed for car owners: off-road parking and no local shops.

There are far more electrical items in homes today than there were in the fifties and sixties. People spend more time watching TV now, and less time cooking and eating together. Children in the fifties and sixties spent more time playing interactive games, and more time out of doors. Today, lack of exercise and excess weight resulting from life style is a serious problem in young people.

Most women who had been working during the war lost their jobs to men returning home and the fifties was a time when women were expected to be homemakers. Stereotypical images of women were seriously challenged by the liberation movement of the late sixties and seventies. Nowadays, while women can consider a wider range of options for career and life style, many go to work and also do domestic chores and child care as well.

Starting Points	Main Activity	Simplified Activity	Extension Activity
B13 *'Shopping'* Talk about the way that cars and big supermarkets have changed shopping habits.	Ask the children to read through the words and phrases in pairs and to discuss how they will use them to write about the way shopping has changed.	Give the children a copy of the sheet with sentence beginnings written on (People did their shopping at ... They travelled by ... or ... and so on). Ask them to complete the sentences.	Give the children copies of maps of their local area or nearest town from 1950 and today. Ask them to find changes in the layout of the town and to mark supermarkets and new housing estates.
B14 *'Inside homes'* Ask the children to think of all the electrical/digital items they have at home. Decide which ones would have been available in the fifties or sixties.	Ask the children to look carefully at the pictures and discuss their comments as a class. Provide, or ask them to bring, catalogues and magazines to show the range of electrical items in homes today.	Ask the children to choose one of the rooms and collect and label the pictures.	Give the children a number of items or pictures of items from the fifties and sixties. Ask them to look at the design and materials used and write a description. Compare with similar items of today.
B15 *'Women'* Talk about the changes for women since 1948. Discuss the way advertisers aim their advertising at a particular type of person.	Ask the children to study and discuss the advertisement in pairs and to share their ideas with the class.	Give the children a copy of the sheet with specific questions about the advertisement and ask them to answer the questions.	Ask the children to prepare questions to ask women (of a suitable age!) about changes since 1948. Invite a visitor to the class or ask the children to interview someone they know.

Plenary

Divide the class into five groups and ask each one to prepare for a revival day and to prepare to act as children living in that decade. On the chosen day, each group (in costume) can present to the class, or a school assembly, aspects of their lives: home, parents' jobs, current events, favourite music, their own aspirations and so on.

Shopping

- Compare shops today with those of the 1950s.

You can use these words:
bomb damage in Second World War, new shopping centre in town, specialist shops (baker, butcher, grocer, greengrocer), corner shops, out-of-town shopping centres, big supermarkets, small shops closing down, cars, buses, freezers, new housing estates

Today

1950s

Inside homes

- Look at the pictures of furniture and electrical goods from the fifties and sixties. Use catalogues and magazines to cut out and stick items for the equivalent room today.

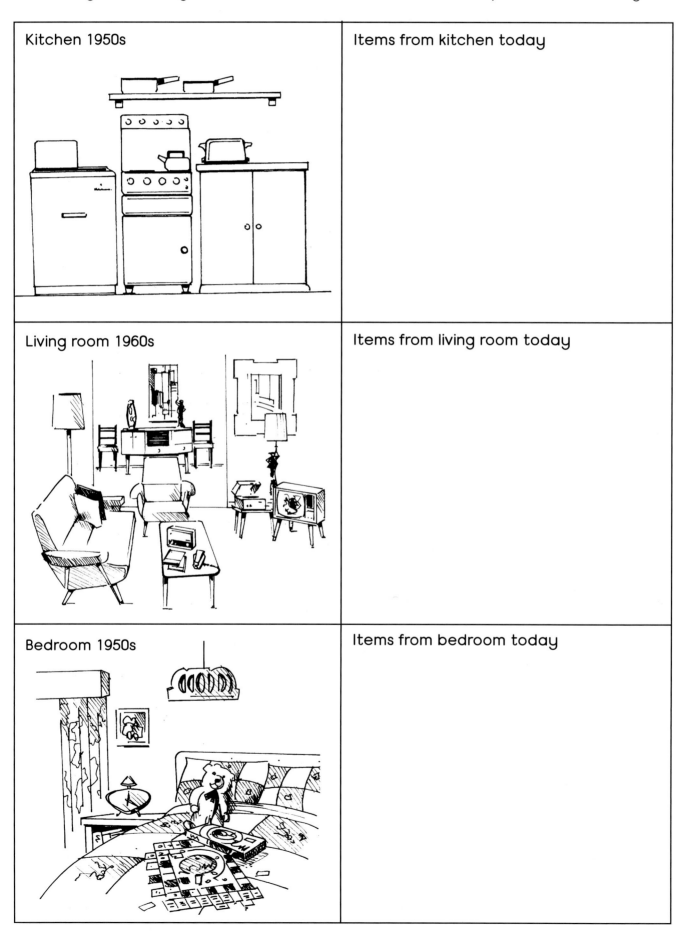

Kitchen 1950s	Items from kitchen today
Living room 1960s	Items from living room today
Bedroom 1950s	Items from bedroom today

Look at this advert from 1950.

Bringing the joys of refrigeration to every home!

New "Family" Frigidaire for only £89.19.0

No other refrigerator gives you so much for so little money. Keeps a whole week's shopping Frigidaire-fresh !

Has your family had to manage without a refrigerator ? You needn't any longer— for here's the new, low-price " Family " Frigidaire ! Now you, too, can protect family health . . . serve tastier meals . . . turn entertaining into fun. You can keep food fresh in any weather, save house-keeping money by avoiding waste, enjoy more leisure. When food keeps till it's needed, once-a-week shopping is ample !

This fine table-top Frigidaire is easy on kitchen space, generous in storage room. Though only 2 ft. square by 3 ft. high, it gives more than 4 cu. ft. of inside storage space — enough for all the family needs !

But the best way to learn about the " Family " Frigidaire is to see it for yourself at Frigidaire Dealers, Electricity Board Service Centres and all large stores.

£89.19.0
including purchase tax and installation
H.P. terms available

Holds enough food for all the family

Top-to-bottom refrigeration—so *no* waste space. All perishable food is kept fresh, wholesome and safe from germs and deterioration. And more food *inside* your refrigerator means more free kitchen and larder space *outside* !

Represents the woman's point of view !

In a country-wide survey by the *Electrical Association for Women*, house-wives listed these features as specially desirable in a refrigerator : work-table top, quiet running, frozen food storage space, compact design.

See how the "Family" Frigidaire scores on these points !

White acid-resistant porcelain table-top with splash back. So durable it won't scratch, chip or stain even when you slice bread or cut meat on it.
Extra quiet " Meter-Miser " power unit—radio and TV suppressed—uses less current than an ordinary light bulb and is backed by a 5-Year Warranty.
Big Super Freezer stores 12 lb. of frozen foods or ice cream.
Frigidaire design produces a marvel of compactness.

Other special features include :—

Quick-Release Ice Tray; Adjustable Cold Control; easily cleaned interior — acid-resistant porcelain lining, rounded corners, removable shelves; all-steel cabinet with 1-Year Warranty; smooth exterior — wipes clean instantly.

You can't match *FRIGIDAIRE*
Regd. Trademark

Made in Britain by
FRIGIDAIRE DIVISION OF GENERAL MOTORS LIMITED
Stag Lane, Kingsbury, London, N.W.9. Telephone : COLindale 6541

● Describe the type of woman the advertisers are trying to attract.

_____

_____

● What has changed for women since 1948?

_____

_____

● What has stayed the same?

_____

_____

Tudor Exploration: Maps and Motives

Learning Objectives

Children should:

■ understand Tudor knowledge of the world and motives for exploration.

■ learn about and the role of Tudor monarchs in relation to explorers.

Background

Coastal maps of Europe were quite accurate in Tudor times, as the area had been explored for centuries. Surveyors were able to map coasts quite accurately from the land. They could even include nautical features, such as underwater sand banks and depth markings, to help ships find safe routes into harbours. The further from Europe the more unreliable the maps became; the poles were unknown territory. The Spanish and Portuguese had conquered most of South and Central America by 1550 and so these areas could not be closely investigated by English ships; cartographers had to depend on Spanish maps. The other continents had not yet been colonised.

Trade and treasure were the main motives for exploring; the treasure stolen from Spain (originally taken from inhabitants of America) made a significant difference to the finances of Elizabeth I. Monarchs were also keen to extend their power and religion to other lands. Today, expeditions are more likely to have a scientific basis and raise money from independent sponsors.

Starting Points	Main Activity	Simplified Activity	Extension Activity
T1 *'The Tudor map of the world'* Talk about how maps are made today and introduce the term 'cartographer'. Discuss how maps were made in Tudor Times.	Give the children time to read about the cartographer; discuss each point. Give the children modern maps of the world for the second part of the task. Either tell them or show a map illustrating the parts of the world conquered by Spain.	Ask the children to compare the Tudor map to a modern one, and shade areas of the Tudor map to indicate either 'similar' or 'different'.	Ask the children to write an account to explain why some areas were better known than others.
T2 *'Reasons for (and against) exploring in Tudor times'* Talk about the reasons that people have for exploring today.	Ask the children to work in pairs to sort the cards and to decide whether they would like to have been explorers or not. Ask individuals to report and explain their decision to the class.	Ask the children to work with a partner who will read and discuss each card with them.	Ask the children to write a letter from a Tudor sea captain to persuade a friend to come on a voyage of exploration with him.
T3 *'Explorers and monarchs'* Explain, in general terms, the extent of power of a Tudor monarch and their relationship to the courtiers.	Read the text with the children and ask questions to make sure that they understand it. Encourage them to describe the possible documents in different words from those of the text. Suggest some phrases that could be used in the full documents.	Make sure that children understand the meaning of the text. Omit the first written task. Give the children a writing frame for one of the documents and ask them to complete it.	Give the children suitable resources and ask them to investigate other Tudor explorers, the monarchs they served, and the relationship between the two.

Plenary

Create a chart with the children to compare a long sea voyage in Tudor times with one today. Use headings such as: maps, knowledge about other places, reasons, relationship with government/monarch, consequences of failure, consequences of success.

The Tudor map of the world

This is where the cartographer got his information from:

1. Skilled surveyors who mapped well-known areas – the most accurate.

2. An educated guess for areas that were completely unknown to English sea captains – the least accurate.

3. Sea captains who had visited parts of the world that were new to the cartographer – quite reliable, but not accurate.

4. Stolen or copied charts or maps of areas where English ships couldn't go because they were controlled by Spain or other countries – not accurate.

Clue: you will need to find out which parts of the world were controlled by Spain in Tudor times.

• Compare the Tudor map below with a modern map of the world. Choose a colour for each of the categories 1–4 above and shade the Tudor map in the relevant colour.

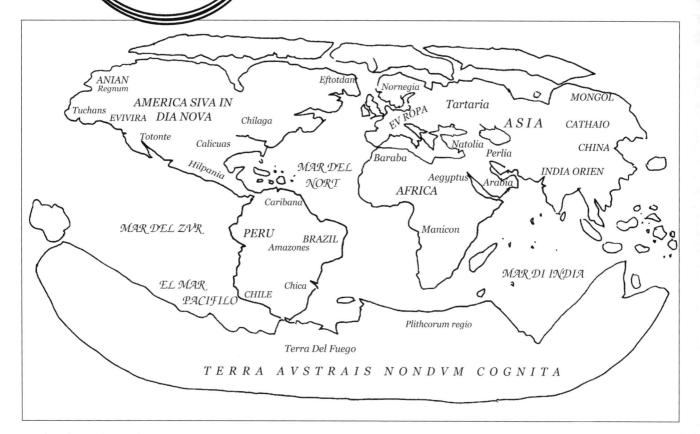

ANIAN Regnum
AMERICA SIVA IN DIA NOVA
Tuchans
EVIVIRA
Chilaga
Eftotdan
Nornegia
EVROPA
Tartaria
MONGOL
ASIA
CATHAIO
Totonte
Calicuas
Natolia
Perlia
CHINA
Hilpania
Baraba
MAR DEL NORT
Aegyptus
Arabia
INDIA ORIEN
AFRICA
Caribana
MAR DEL ZVR
PERU
BRAZIL
Amazones
Manicon
MAR DI INDIA
EL MAR PACIFILO
CHILE
Chica
Plithcorum regio
Terra Del Fuego
TERRA AVSTRAIS NONDVM COGNITA

Reasons for (and against) exploring in Tudor times

● You are a Tudor sea captain. Will you explore outside Europe? Cut out and sort the cards into for and against, then decide.

You might find some people to trade with. For example, you fill your ship with goods (wool, leather, metals). You find a place that has something that is valuable in England (spices). You swap goods, bring back the spices and sell them.

You will need a good pilot to help you find the way in unknown waters. Even then, you might get lost, or go a long way off route.

Your sailors might get fed up and gang up on you. This is called mutiny.

You might come across a Spanish ship with treasure on board from South America. You can capture the ship and take all the treasure.

You could find a wonderful new land where crops grow well and the inhabitants are friendly. People from England could go and settle there.

You have to take a lot of food on a long voyage and you don't always find places to get more. You might run out of supplies and fresh water.

Illness is very common on ships. The sailors get ill because their diet is not good. Also, you are at risk of catching 'foreign' diseases in other parts of the world, and you have no immunity to them.

If you discover new places, people to trade with, or bring back treasure, you will be famous and get a reward from the king or queen.

Explorers and monarchs

In Tudor times the king or queen was very involved in the activities of explorers. Explorers were rewarded if they brought back wealth and fame. They could be punished if they failed.

In 1578 Walter Raleigh sailed with his half-brother Humphrey Gilbert. They had Queen Elizabeth's permission to search for new lands, not owned by 'Christian princes'. ① The expedition failed because of bad weather and illness. The Queen's Council forbade them to sail again. ②

In 1583 Raleigh was a favourite of the Queen and she gave him a Bishop's palace in London. ③ In 1585 she knighted him for his plans to establish a colony in the Americas. However, in 1592 she had him arrested because he had got married without her permission. ④

She kept his wife in the Tower of London for a few months, but let her out after Raleigh helped in giving her a big share of some treasure stolen from Spanish ships. ⑤

- Where you see this symbol describe the letter or document that could have been written for the event.

1. *A certificate to say that Gilbert was allowed to take new lands in the name of the Queen and signed by the Queen.*

2. _____

3. _____

4. _____

5. _____

- Choose one of the documents and write it in full on a sheet of paper.

Tudor Ships

Learning Objectives

Children should:
- learn about the construction and operation of Tudor ships.
- learn about navigation in Tudor times.

Background

Tudor ships were broad, slow and difficult to manoeuvre. The sails were made of canvas and the ropes of hemp. Francis Drake's ship, the Golden Hind, weighed 100 tons, had five decks, 18 guns, and a crew of about 170. It was 75 feet (22.6 m) long and 20 feet (6.1 m) wide. Only a small selection of crew is illustrated on page 66. The carpenter and barber surgeon would have their own cabin, as well as the captain. Other specialist crew included gunners, trumpeters, drummer, quarter-master and purser.

The Tudor navigator had a range of instruments for navigation, only a few of which are illustrated on page 67. He had instruments to measure how far north/south the ship was (latitude), but none to calculate how far east/west (longitude) it was. To do this he had to measure the speed and direction of the ship and use dead reckoning. There were no telescopes, so known landmarks on the coast (churches, cliffs and so on) were used.

Starting Points	Main Activity	Simplified Activity	Extension Activity
T4 *'A Tudor ship'* Show the children pictures of Tudor ships at sea. Talk about how they were constructed and their manoeuvrability.	Ask the children to look at the picture of the ship and to complete the text. Then ask them to discuss in pairs what they would like to find out about Tudor ships before writing their list of questions.	Omit the gap-filling activity. Give the children a number of headings (*Food and water, sailors sleeping arrangements, how the ship worked*) and ask them to write questions about each one.	Give the children suitable resources; then ask them to find answers to some of the questions they have written and report their findings to the class.
T5 *'Crew and cargo'* Talk about the operation of Tudor ships, how they worked, the jobs to be done and the size of the crew.	Give the children copies of pages 65 (enlarged onto A3) and 66. Ask them to look at the pictures and read the instructions on page 66 in pairs. Allow time for them to ask questions before they draw the figures onto the ship on page 65.	Ask the children to work with a partner who will help them to find the location, on page 65, of each of the items on page 66.	Ask the children to imagine being the captain of a merchant ship and to write an account of the preparations for their voyage.
T6 *'The ship's instruments'* Discuss the information that a Tudor navigator would need. Ask the children if they can think of ways to measure the things without modern instruments.	Ask the children to read the text and look at the pictures in pairs, before putting a number next to each picture. As a class, discuss the purpose of the instruments, then ask the children to complete the sentences individually.	Give the children simple sentences to match to each picture. (The sand runs through the glass; it times one hour. The needle points north. And so on.)	Give the children suitable materials and ask them to make their own sounding line to measure the depth of water.

Plenary

Ask the children to recall vocabulary connected with Tudor ships and sailing. Work with them to compile a glossary of terms.

A Tudor ship

- Complete the sentences using the words in the box below.

| bad   sails   rudder   bunks   turn   wood |

Ships in Tudor times were made of ————,
usually oak. They had huge ———— to catch
the wind, and a ———— to steer the ship.
Compared to sailing boats today, they were slow
and difficult to ———— around. The captain
and the officers had ———— to sleep in but
the sailors slept on the deck, or found shelter below in
———— weather.

- What do you want to find out about Tudor ships?
  Write a list of questions.

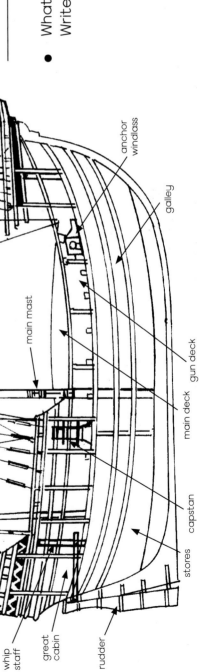

foremast

main mast

anchor
windlass

galley

gun deck

main deck

capstan

stores

poop
deck

whip
staff

great
cabin

rudder

Crew and cargo

● Add these details to the ship on activity sheet T4.

Put the crates of food, and barrels of water and beer in the stores.

Fill the very bottom (under the stores) with rocks, for ballast (to balance the ship).

Put the canons on the gun deck.

Put the longboat on the main deck.

Put in three men to operate the anchor windlass.
Put in three men to turn the capstan, to hoist the main sail.

Put the captain in the great cabin.

Put the helmsman next to the whip staff (the vertical stick connected to the rudder).

Put the cook and his cook pot in the galley.

Put the sail menders and sails in the room at the bottom of the foremast.

Put the pilot on the poop deck.

FOLENS HISTORY IN ACTION 5

The ship's instruments

- Match the instrument to the description.

1. A long piece of rope with a lead weight attached. It had knots and pieces of leather to mark the distance (like a ruler). This was thrown overboard and lowered until the weight touched the sea bed, just under the ship.

2. A very long reel of string with knots tied at even distances and a piece of wood on the end. The line was reeled out at the same speed as the ship moved and the time between the knots was timed with a sand glass.

3. A magnetic needle in a case. The needle always pointed north.

4. A glass container with sand inside, and a very narrow middle. The sand would take exactly one hour to run from the top to the bottom. It had to be turned over immediately.

5. A long piece of wood with four moveable cross-pieces at right angles. It was held up to the eye so that one of the horizontal pieces touched the sun at one end and the horizon at the other end. The navigator then measured the distance of the cross-piece from his eye.

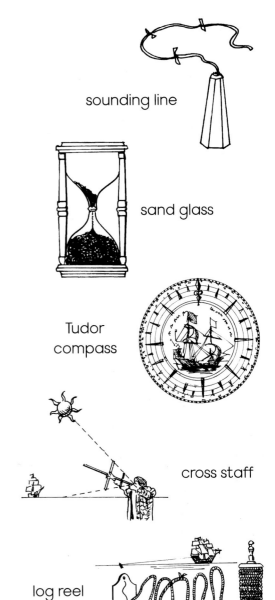

sounding line

sand glass

Tudor compass

cross staff

log reel

- Use these words to finish the sentences:

> depth of the water   speed of the ship   direction of the ship
> time   how far north or south the ship was

The sand glass measured the _____ .

The compass told them the _____ .

The cross staff told them _____ .

The log reel measured the _____ .

The sounding line measured the _____ .

Francis Drake

Learning Objectives

Children should:

- learn about conditions for sailors on board a Tudor ship.
- know the route and the results of Drake's circumnavigation of the world.
- consider the different possible interpretations of Drake's exploits.

Background

As a result of the conditions and diet on Tudor ships, half of the crew may have died on a long voyage. There were cases of mutiny when sailors were under pressure. Drake was apparently a good captain who inspired loyalty.

After sailing up the west coast of the Americas, Drake wanted to find the elusive North–West passage back to England, but gave up. He did not initially set out to sail around the world.

Drake's own account and notes on the voyage were suppressed because of his piracy and for fear of further antagonising Spain. The account of the voyage was compiled later.

Starting Points	Main Activity	Simplified Activity	Extension Activity
T7 *'Conditions for Tudor sailors'* Talk to the children about the problems of storing food, the cause of scurvy and the reasons for discipline on a Tudor ship.	Allow time for the children to read the information, ask questions and make comments. Discuss possible entries in the captain's log before asking them to write their own.	Give the children a list of questions (What did sailors drink? What was the punishment for swearing? And so on.). Ask them to find the answers.	Ask the children to use this information, combined with the information about ships on pages 65 and 66, to write an imaginative account of a young sailor's first voyage.
T8 and **T9** *'The circumnavigation'* and *'Map of Drake's voyage, 1577–80'* Look again at the Tudor map of the world and a modern map. Talk about the knowledge of sailors at the time.	Ask the children to work through the text, marking the route on the map as they go. Ask them to compare with a partner when they have finished.	Give the children a list of the places on the route and a map on which the route has been partially drawn. Ask them to complete it.	Give the children a more detailed account of the circumnavigation (or read one to them). Ask them to make notes or draw pictures on their map to record key incidents.
T10 *'Results of the voyage'* Talk about the reasons Drake had for making the voyage.	Ask the children to read through the text in pairs and agree on the correct headings. Ask individuals to report back.	Give the children a sentence for each result (Drake was rich/poor after the voyage. The Queen was angry/pleased … and so on). Ask them to underline the correct word.	Ask the children to write a report of Drake's return to England after the voyage, in the style of a sensationalist newspaper.
T11 *'Pirate, explorer or admiral?'* Show the children a picture of Francis Drake. Talk about the different reputations famous people can have depending on the position of the observer.	Allow time for the children to read the notes. Discuss ways in which the evidence could be differently interpreted before asking then to write two versions of Drake's biography on a separate sheet of paper.	Give the children a copy of the sheet on which the biographies have been written but with missing words. Ask them to complete the text.	Give the children suitable resources. Ask them to investigate Drake's life in more detail and to report their findings to the class.

Plenary

Choose a group of children to play Drake and some of his sailors. Ask the rest of the class to prepare questions. Provide some costumes, if possible, and conduct the interview as if in Tudor times.

Conditions for Tudor sailors

● Use the following information to write, on a separate sheet, extracts from the Captain's log about his crew.

The symptoms of scurvy

No energy, boils on the skin, swollen and bleeding gums, and teeth falling out. After nine days legs and arms become swollen, black bruises appear, can't breathe, coma and then death.

Typical daily ration

Either: 0.5 kg ships biscuits
4.5 litres beer
113 g fish
57 g butter
113 g cheese

or: 0.5 kg biscuits
4.5 litres beer
1 kg beef

Hygiene

There were no washing facilities and the toilet was a plank over the sea. Sailors had head lice and fleas. They only had one set of clothes. Rats were common on ships.

Punishments for sailors

For swearing: spike in the mouth.
For stealing: covered in tar and feathers and then 'running the gauntlet' of the crew.
For drawing a knife on another crew member: loss of hand.
Worst punishment: keel-hauling (tied to a rope, thrown over one side, hauled under ship and up other side – most sailors died after this).
For murder: thrown overboard, tied to the dead body.

Storing food

Ships were at sea for a long time. Food had to be dried, salted or pickled. Fruit easily went rotten. Some ships took live animals. Many sailors became ill or died because of the poor diet.

The circumnavigation

- Read the description of Drake's voyage and mark his route on the map on activity sheet T9.

November 1577 Drake left Plymouth, England, with five ships. They had to return because of storms.

December 1577 They set sail again and reached the coast of Morocco. They took more food and a small ship.

Next they went to the Cape Verde Islands, and got ready to cross the Atlantic. They reached Brazil and sailed down the coast of South America.

June 1578 At the River Plate, Argentina, Drake disposed of two of the ships and had one man tried and executed for mutiny. Drake rallied his men.

August 1578 They arrived at the entry to the Straits of Magellan where Drake renamed his ship the *Golden Hind*. The three ships sailed through the Straits into the Pacific.

September 1578 In terrible storms the *Marigold* sank and the *Elizabeth* was blown back into the straits and returned to England.

Drake continued up the coast of Chile, stealing treasure from Spanish ships.

April 1579 He stopped for repairs at an island (Cano) near south Mexico.

June 1579 He sailed west and then north, looking for a way home to the North West. Eventually they stopped at a bay somewhere off the coast of North America. The exact location has never been found. It might have been in California. They stayed there for five weeks and had good relations with the inhabitants.

Drake realised that they would have to go westwards. From America they sailed west across the Pacific and came to the Pelew Islands, then Ternate, Indonesia and finally the Spice Islands.

January 1580 The ship was grounded on a reef, but was then blown off again and they continued to Java.

They crossed the Indian Ocean, went round the Cape of Good Hope into the Atlantic and up the coast of Africa.

Autumn 1580 The *Golden Hind* arrived in England in the autumn. They had been away for three years and had travelled 36 000 miles.

Map of Drake's voyage, 1577–80

• Read the description of the route on activity sheet T8 and mark it on the map.

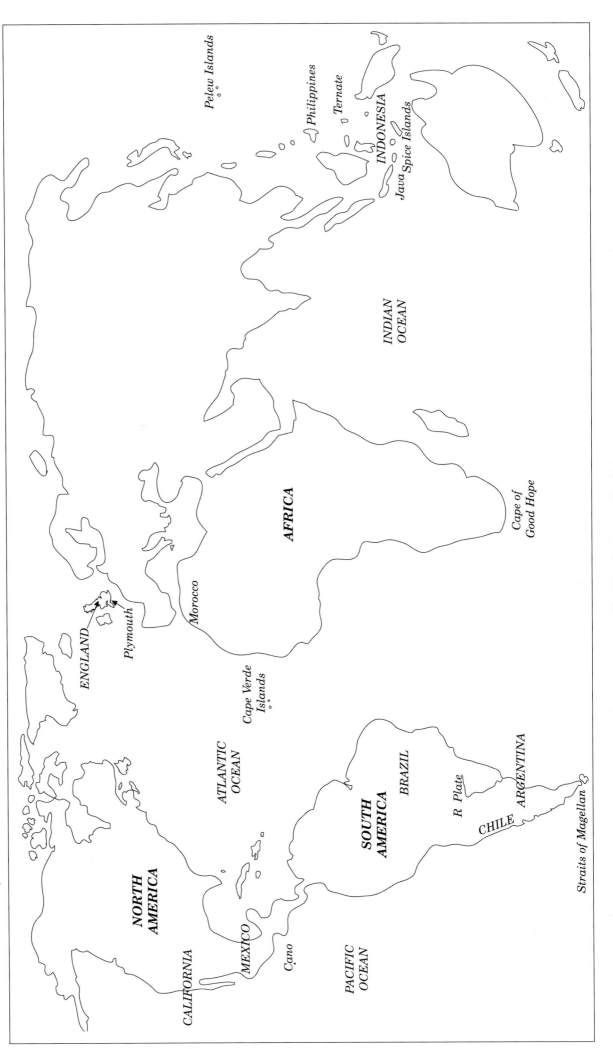

NORTH AMERICA

CALIFORNIA

MEXICO

Cano

PACIFIC OCEAN

SOUTH AMERICA

BRAZIL

R. Plate

CHILE

ARGENTINA

Straits of Magellan

ATLANTIC OCEAN

Cape Verde Islands

ENGLAND

Plymouth

Morocco

AFRICA

Cape of Good Hope

INDIAN OCEAN

Pelew Islands

Philippines

Ternate

INDONESIA

Java Spice Islands

Results of the voyage

- Choose the best heading from the boxes below for each of the results of the voyage.

'Discovery of new animals'	'Personal wealth'
'Worse relations with Spain'	'New knowledge about the world'
'Favour with the Queen'	'More trade for England'

The treasure that Drake's ship brought back was estimated to be worth £600 000 (£25 million today). Drake was a rich man.

Queen Elizabeth took half of the treasure. She had Drake knighted. She did not punish him for piracy, even though the Spanish King wanted her to.

Philip II, King of Spain, was very angry about Drake stealing his treasure. He did not declare war straight away; instead he waited for an excuse.

Some accounts of the voyage say that when Drake was blown off course after the Straits of Magellan, he discovered that there was open water to the south of Chile.

"Amongst other things which we had of them, the sheep of the country were most memorable. Their height and length was like a cow, and their strength good for their size ...These sheep have necks like camels; their heads bearing a reasonable resemblance to other sheep. The Spaniards use them to great profit. Their wool is exceedingly fine, their flesh good meat. They carry, over the mountains, heavy loads, for 300 leagues together."

Adapted from *The World Encompassed* by Francis Drake's nephew (also called Francis Drake)

They made a treaty (deal) with the Sultan of Ternate. He said they could sell their goods, and buy things from him to take back to England.

Pirate, explorer or admiral?

- Use these notes to write two versions of Drake's biography: one by an English writer and one by a Spanish writer.

born around 1540 in Devon

father a preacher to sailors in the navy, not wealthy

family lived in the hulk of an old ship

first voyage at sea, in the 1550s, as apprentice to master of small cargo ship

master left the ship to Drake in his will

became sea captain, trading and taking treasure from Spanish and Portuguese ships

when he was a young sailor after storm in Gulf of Mexico, the Spanish gave him permission to land, then attacked, killing many sailors, Drake escaped, shocked by actions of Spanish

voyage all the way around the world made him rich and famous, treasure taken from Spanish ships and ports

commanded English fleet against Spanish Armada

died of a tropical disease on an expedition against Spanish in Caribbean, 1596

buried at sea

married twice but no children

FOLENS HISTORY IN ACTION 5

The Colonies

Learning Objectives

Children should:
- understand some of the motives for creating a new settlement in America.
- learn about the activities of the first settlers and how the settlement failed.

Background

In 1578 Sir Humphrey Gilbert, Raleigh's half-brother was given the first patent from the Queen to 'inhabit and possess' new lands; Raleigh went with him on his first voyage. Gilbert died on a second voyage and the patent was later given to Raleigh. Initially there were ideas of using a new settlement as a base for forays against French and Spanish shipping, which would pay for the expense of a colony. The possibilities of gold and copper mines and lucrative cash crops were an incentive. Gilbert had the idea of putting 'needy people' to work. Only men were recruited and apparently selected for building skills. Religion was important; this was an opportunity to spread Christianity (the Protestant version) to other lands.

It is generally agreed that the settlers went wrong in depending on the indigenous people for food, and in the way that they treated them. The first reports of a land of plenty were written from observations of the summer months. In winter and spring food became scarce. Although initially good, relations between the settlers and the native islanders deteriorated, partly because of the food issue but also, it seems, due to misunderstandings, over-suspicion and over-reactions on the part of the English. They regularly took prisoners to get information.

Starting Points	Main Activity	Simplified Activity	Extension Activity
T12 *'Roanoke Island, 1584'* Explain to the children how the initiative for the settlement came about, and the motives behind it.	Read the extracts with the children and explain new vocabulary. Ask individuals to give examples of reasons from the extracts, before asking the class to make a list of the reasons why Roanoke was a good place to settle.	Give the children a list of the reasons (plenty of food, plenty of fish, good soil … and so on). Ask them to match the reasons to the extracts.	Ask the children to write an imaginative account of meeting the settlers, from the point of view of the indigenous people.
T13 and **T14** *'Settlement on Roanoke Island (1) and (2)'* On a map, show the location of Roanoke. Talk about the preparations, the skills and supplies needed to start a colony in Tudor times.	Explain that everyone has the same text, but A and B have different missing information. Pair children with the same sheet to read through the text and write the questions needed to fill in the missing information. Change the pairs to ask and answer the questions to complete the sheets.	Ask the children to work with a partner who will read the text with them, and help them to write the questions. Give them a copy that has the phrases needed for answers underlined.	Ask the children to combine what they have learned so far to produce a first-hand account of the expedition from the point of view of Lane, in the form of a diary and sketches.

Plenary

Using the experience of the first settlers, ask the children to compile a list of advice for the second group of settlers, who went the following year.

Roanoke Island, 1584

Arthur Barlowe was one of two captains sent by Walter Raleigh to explore new lands in preparation for a settlement. He found a good place at Roanoke Island.

● Read the extracts from his account and make a list of the reasons why Roanoke was a good place to settle.

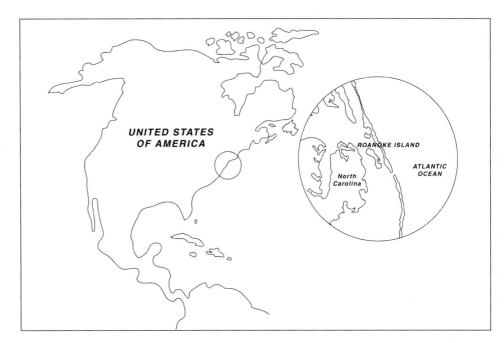

We viewed the land about us, where we first landed, very sandy and low towards the waters side, but so full of grapes, that the very beating and surge of the Sea overflowed them

He [an inhabitant of the island] fell to fishing, and in less then half an hour, he had filled his boat with as many fish as it could hold …

This Island had many goodly woods full of Deer, Conies [rabbits], Hares, and Fowl, even in the midst of Summer in incredible abundance. The woods are not such as you find in Bohemia, Moscovia, or Hercynia, barren and fruitless, but the highest and reddest Cedars in the world …

The next day there came to us several boats, and in one of them the King's brother, accompanied with forty or fifty men, very handsome and goodly people, and in their behaviour as mannerly and civil as any in Europe.

We exchanged our tin dish for twenty skins, worth twenty Crowns … And a copper kettle for fifty skins worth fifty Crowns. They offered us good exchange for our hatchets, and axes, and for knives, and would have given anything for swords: but we would not part with any.

The soil is the most plentiful, sweet, fruitful and wholesome of all the world: there are above fourteen sweet smelling timber trees, and the most part of their underwoods are Bays, and such like: they have those Oaks that we have, but far greater and better.

We were entertained with all love and kindness, and generosity. We found the people most gentle, loving, and faithful, void of all guile and treason…The people only care how to defend themselves from the cold in their short winter, and to feed themselves with such food as the soil will provide…

Settlement on Roanoke Island (1)

Text for pupil A

Read about the settlers, write questions to find out the missing information and prepare to answer questions from your partner.

The expedition to establish a colony was led by _____. He took seven ships and 500 men. One hundred and eight of them were colonists. They arrived near Roanoke Island on _____. Grenville stayed a short while, and then returned to England for supplies, leaving Ralph Lane as the governor of the colonists.

They were mostly men skilled in a practical trade. (There were no women). They built a fort shaped like a star, and houses made of _____; with thatched roofs. Some of the men explored the coast. Thomas Hariot collected information about plants, animals and minerals. _____ made drawings of the islanders and the animals and plants. The colonists learned how to smoke tobacco in pipes.

At first they had good relations with Chief Winiga and his tribe. They arranged for the islanders to supply them with food. By the spring of 1586 the situation had changed. At this time of year there was not enough food and the tribe stopped supplying them. They stole from the islanders' fish traps. By June they were at war with the Indians and in one of the battles, the Chief was killed.

The colonists were in trouble. Grenville was late in returning with supplies. On 9 June the news came that Francis Drake was nearby with a fleet of 23 ships. Drake offered to _____. Lane wanted to take some supplies and a ship, and wait a bit longer, but the first ship Drake gave him was blown out to sea, and the second was too big for the harbour, so they all returned to England.

_____ weeks later Grenville arrived and searched in vain for the colonists. He wanted to preserve the colony for his Queen and country, so he left 15 men there with enough supplies for two years and returned to England.

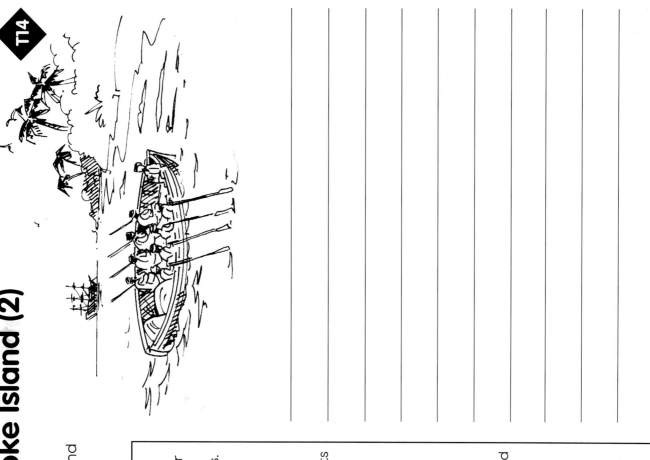

Settlement on Roanoke Island (2)

Text for pupil B

Read about the settlers, write questions to find out the missing information and prepare to answer questions from your partner.

The expedition to establish a colony was led by Sir Richard Grenville. He took seven ships and 500 men. _____ of them were colonists. They arrived near Roanoke Island on 27 July 1585. Grenville stayed a short while, then returned to England for supplies, leaving _____ as the governor of the colonists.

They were mostly men skilled in a practical trade. (There were no women). They built a fort shaped like a _____, and houses made of bricks, or perhaps wood, with thatched roofs. Some of the men explored the coast. _____ collected information about plants, animals and minerals. John White made drawings of the islanders and the animals and plants. The colonists learned how to smoke tobacco in pipes.

At first they had good relations with Chief Winiga and his tribe. They arranged for the islanders to supply them with food. By the spring of 1586 the situation had changed. At this time of year there was not enough food and the tribe stopped supplying them. They stole from the islanders' fish traps. By June they were at war with the Indians and in one of the battles, the Chief was _____ .

The colonists were in trouble. Grenville was late in returning with supplies. On 9 June the news came that Francis Drake was nearby with a fleet of 23 ships. Drake offered to take them back to England. Lane wanted to take some supplies and a ship, and wait a bit longer, but the first ship Drake gave him was blown out to sea, and the second was _____ , so they all returned to England.

Two weeks later Grenville arrived and searched in vain for the colonists. He wanted to preserve the colony for his Queen and country, so he left _____ men there with enough supplies for two years and returned to England.

© Folens (copiable page)   FOLENS HISTORY IN ACTION 5   77

Life in the Colonies

Learning Objectives

Children should:
- learn that John White's paintings tell us about the indigenous people of Roanoke Island.
- know the story of the second settlement and how it is different from the first.

Background

John White was a participant of the first settlement on Roanake Island in 1585 and returned as governor of the second settlement in 1587. His paintings, in watercolour, were intended to make the new land attractive so that more settlers would want to go.

The natives of Roanoke Island lived by hunting and fishing. Their villages were defended with a circle of pointed wooden stakes. The largest village had 30 shelters. The shelters were draped with grass matting, which they rolled up to let in light and air. The couple pictured on page 79 are eating boiled corn from a large wooden plate. The English reported that the islanders never ate or drank excessively. In the third illustration people are spearing fish with long sharpened poles. One man is paddling while the other collects the fish. A man and woman are smoking them on a fire.

The second colony had a different rationale from the first. It was to be more civilian than military. This time the settlers would provide their own food by farming the land. Some women and children were included. The reason for staying at Roanoke rather than continuing to Chesapeake as planned is attributed by some sources to a dispute between White and the ship's captain. See page 80 for details on how the settlers disappeared. Raleigh continued efforts to trace these missing settlers until 1602, when he sent an expedition to look for them. In 1607 a successful colony was established at Jamestown and the inhabitants tried hard to find out from the native Americans what had happened, but no substantial evidence has ever materialised.

Starting Points	Main Activity	Simplified Activity	Extension Activity
T15 *'John White's paintings of the Roanoke people'* Explain White's brief as artist/naturalist of the first settlement. If possible look at some more colour reproductions of his work.	Ask the children to look at the drawings in pairs and to make as many observations as possible. Encourage them to ask questions (some of which you may be unable to answer). Ask them to write descriptions individually.	Begin in the same way as for the main activity. Ask the children to write words or phrases next to each picture to describe what they see.	Give the children access to White's paintings of animals and plants. Ask them to choose one and write a description from the point of view of a person in Tudor times, seeing the plant or animal for the first time.
T16 *'The second settlement on Roanoke Island'* Explain the different intention for the second colony. Discuss why settling in a different area would be a good idea.	Allow time for the children to read the text in silence. Ask questions to check and aid understanding. Discuss ways to illustrate the text.	Ask a child with a good understanding of the story to tell it to the others. For the simplified task ask the children to draw and label three pictures for the beginning, middle and end of the story.	Ask the children to write a theory about what could have happened to the settlers and to give reasons.

Plenary

Draw a timeline from 1584 to 1590 and ask the children to contribute the main events of the first expedition and two settlements on Roanoke.

John White's paintings of the Roanoke people

Use these sketches of John White's paintings to describe the islanders and their life.

_____

_____

_____

_____

_____

_____

_____

_____

_____

_____

_____

_____

_____

_____

_____

_____

_____

_____

_____

_____

_____

• Draw pictures to illustrate the text.

1. In 1587 Raleigh organised a second expedition. This time there were 150 people, including 17 women and nine children. They were to be given land and they were called 'planters'. He wanted them to go to Chesapeake Bay, about 130 miles north of Roanoke, because there was a better harbour and better conditions for settling. Three ships set sail from Plymouth on 8 May.	5. The Croatoans told them that the people of Dasamonquepeuc had killed Grenville's men. White and Captain Stafford and 24 men attacked the village, but the inhabitants had already gone and, instead, ended up attacking the Croatoans who had gone to the village to look for food left behind. Manteo persuaded the Croatoans to forgive the English.
2. They arrived in July. John White was the governor of this expedition and he went to Roanoke to look for the 15 men who had been left behind by Grenville. He and a small group of planters searched the place where the men had been left, but found only the bones of one man.	6. As a reward for helping them, Manteo was christened and declared Lord of Roanoke.
3. The next day they walked to the fort and houses of the first settlement. The fort had been destroyed, but the houses were still standing. The back rooms were overgrown; they found deer feeding inside. They lost hope of finding Grenville's men.	7. The planters needed more supplies; Governor White was to go back to England to get them. Before he left they discussed moving the colony, and they agreed to leave a sign to say where they were if they did move. They would leave a cross to show if they had been forced away. White left on 27 August.
4. The settlers stayed at Roanoke instead of going on to Chesapeake. We don't know why. The inhabitants of Roanoke Island were not friendly to the settlers but they made friends with the Croatoans on another island, with the help of an Indian called Manteo.	8. It was three years before White returned! The war with Spain meant that all the ships were being used and it was difficult to cross the sea. When he eventually landed he found the planters gone, the letters CRO carved in Roman letters on a tree on a hill. They went to the old settlement and found the houses had been taken down and a barricade of tree trunks had been put up round the area. On one of the trunks they found the word CROATOAN. They didn't find a cross.

9. White planned to go to Croatoan but the weather did not allow him to and eventually he had to return to England. There were many attempts to find out what really happened to 'the lost colony', but it remains an unsolved mystery.